SHADOW BALL

PITT POETRY SERIES

Ed Ochester, Editor

SHADOW BALL

NEW AND SELECTED POEMS

Charles Harper Webb

UNIVERSITY OF PITTSBURGH PRESS

Published by the University of Pittsburgh Press, Pittsburgh, Pa., 15260

Manufactured in the United States of America

Printed on acid-free paper

10 9 8 7 6 5 4 3 2 1

ISBN 13: 978-08229-6042-3

ISBN 10: 0-8229-6042-7

FOR KAREN AND ERIK

Contents

from *Tulip Farms and Leper Colonies*   2001

from *Hot Popsicles*   2005

from *Amplified Dog*   2006

New Poems

from *Reading the Water*   1997

The Mummy Meets Hot-Headed Naked Ice-Borers

Djedmaatesankh—temple musician, wife of Paankhntof,
daughter of Shedtaope—died childless, aged
thirty-five, in the tenth century BC, of blood
poisoning from an abscessed incisor. CAT scans
of her mummy show how the abscess chewed
a walnut-sized hole in her upper jaw, gnawing

bone the way the creatures called "hot-headed
naked ice-borers" gnaw tunnels through
Antarctic ice. Six inches long, hairless and pink,
they look in pictures like sea lions with tumors
on their foreheads, and saber-teeth. The teeth
chew tunnels; the "tumors" are lumps of bone,

the skin of which writhes with blood vessels
radiating heat. Their normal temperature
is 110 degrees. Djedmaatesankh's fever
may have reached 104. One shot of penicillin
could have saved her, but it was 3000 years away.
Knowing about ice-borers might have saved French

explorer Philippe Poisson, who disappeared in 1837.
Five foot six, he could have been a large penguin:
the ice-borers' favorite food. A pack collects
under a penguin and, with their foreheads,
melt the ice it's standing on. The penguin sinks
as in quicksand; the borers attack like piranha,

leaving behind only beak, feathers, and feet—
as if the bird has taken them off before bed. Think

of Poisson, torn into fragments by their fangs.
Think of Djedmaatesankh in the three weeks the abscess
took to kill her. How did her husband feel,
hearing her groan? Watching her corpse carried

to the embalmers? Seeing the molded likeness
of her face rise from her pupal coffin? Did he weep
to lose his only love? Was he relieved
that he could remarry, and possibly have sons?
Or had mistresses provided those?
Did his wife's death make him curse, thank, cease

believing in his gods? Did Poisson's wife in Paris
dream of penguin beaks, feathers, feet encased
in ice? Did she see pink squirming things
with Philippe's face? The first night Djedmaatesankh
went to bed with a toothache, did she dream
she was in a room crowded with people in strange clothes,

and while a white-skinned boy stared down at her
and, through a transparent wall like frozen air, made
noises that sounded like "Eeoo, gross," his sister screamed,
and had to be carried outside, and that night
dreamed of Djedmaatesankh walking toward her,
gauze dripping from her shriveled, childless hands?

The Death of Santa Claus

He's had chest pains for weeks,
but doctors don't make house
calls to the North Pole,

he's let his Blue Cross lapse,
blood tests make him faint,
hospital gowns always flap

open, waiting rooms upset
his stomach, and it's only
indigestion anyway, he thinks,

until, feeding the reindeer,
he feels as if a monster fist
has grabbed his heart and won't

stop squeezing. He can't
breathe, and the beautiful white
world he loves goes black,

and he drops on his jelly belly
in the snow and Mrs. Claus
tears out of the toy factory

wailing, and the elves wring
their little hands, and Rudolph's
nose blinks like a sad ambulance

light, and in a tract house
in Houston, Texas, I'm eight,
telling my mom that stupid

kids at school say Santa's a big
fake, and she sits with me
on our purple-flowered couch,

and takes my hand, tears
in her throat, the terrible
news rising in her eyes.

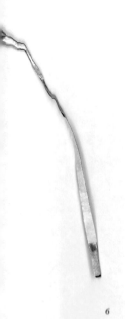

Prayer for the Man Who Mugged My Father, 72

May there be an afterlife.

May you meet him there, the same age as you.
May the meeting take place in a small, locked room.

May the bushes where you hid be there again, leaves tipped with razor-
    blades and acid.
May the rifle butt you bashed him with be in his hands.
May the glass in his car window, which you smashed as he sat stopped
    at a red light, spike the rifle butt, and the concrete on which you'll
    fall.

May the needles the doctors used to close his eye, stab your pupils
    every time you hit the wall and then the floor, which will be often.
May my father let you cower for a while, whimpering, "Please don't
    shoot me. Please."
May he laugh, unload your gun, toss it away;
Then may he take you with bare hands.

May those hands, which taught his son to throw a curve and drive a nail
    and hold a frog, feel like cannonballs against your jaw.
May his arms, which powered handstands and made their muscles jump
    to please me, wrap your head and grind your face like stone.
May his chest, thick and hairy as a bear's, feel like a bear's snapping
    your bones.
May his feet, which showed me the flutter kick and carried me miles
    through the woods, feel like axes crushing your one claim to man-
    hood as he chops you down.

And when you are down, and he's done with you, which will be soon,
    since, even one-eyed, with brain damage, he's a merciful man,

May the door to the room open and let him stride away to the Valhalla
    he deserves.
May you—bleeding, broken—drag yourself upright.

May you think the worst is over;
You've survived, and may still win.

Then may the door open once more, and let me in.

Spiders

They drift through darkness, eight-fingered
hands grasping for your eyes.

In daylight they occur like accidents,
suddenly *there*. They are fear's footprint

on the shower floor, its rune stamped
on the wall. Small, hopping nightmares,

scuttling aliens, they charge at you
with scrabbly legs, jaws dripping pain.

Masters of treachery, they leap from hiding,
paralyze their prey, then suck it dry.

Creeping out from dusty corners, cracks in walls,
they are your landlords when the lights die.

Fuzzy succubae, they sleep with you;
leave itchy kisses where they've been.

Walking to the bathroom, 2 a.m., your feet tickle.
Don't hit the light switch. Don't look down.

It's not enough to spray them with Black Flag;
they must be drowned in it.

It's not enough to crush one gently.
Grind it underfoot until it disappears.

Yet they are beautiful: furry as buffalo,
long-limbed as ballerinas.

Tiny illusionists, they rise and fall
on invisible sky-wires.

Millions of years after crawling from the sea,
they throw out nets to harvest the breeze.

They weave blankets for the ground's feet,
shawls for the quivering shoulders of the trees.

Their webs, transparent fielders' gloves,
pluck flies out of midair.

In this world they helped create, I am the newcomer
threatening, "Get out of town by dawn."

Yet—elfin bodyguards—they clear a path for me
through the constant crush of bugs;

they cordon off a spot—my private tuffet—
and they run away when I sit down.

The Crane Boy

Extreme isolation in early childhood causes
children to have little or no speech
and severely limited mental abilities.

From *Psychology*, by Lester A. Lefton

He was not named for the bird—slow-flying,
legs like jointed straws—but for the long-necked
monsters, squeaky-tongued, that tear tenements down.
Reek! Reek! he cries, and slams his head against
the clinic door. He wants some moldy bread,

a cracked soap dish, sky blue. (Who knows
if this is true? The party guest who said his name—
I forget hers—forgot what else she knew
about him, brother to the Teheran Ape-Child,
Lithuanian Bear-Child, Irish Sheep-Child,

Salzburg Sow-Girl—all those abandoned
by their kind, who, as another kind, survived.)
I see him chained to a commode
in a brownstone condemned and left standing.
Red jelly from his father's head spreads

on the street after a crack deal goes bust.
His mother clamps a charm between her thighs
to restore virginity. Rain rubs its cheek
against his window as he watches the cranes
batter buildings down. No one speaks to him;

but Wernicke's area, Broca's area
spark and sputter in the stinking dark.
Reek! Reek!—far back in his throat,

as if the sounds have fluttered over city blocks
or dropped from clouds like spiders on silk strands.

Maybe he means, *Don't hit me.* Who knows
what he means: shit-glazed, back hunched, arms flapping,
head battering the wall. Maybe it isn't
what I think: pain of a man strapped down waiting
for cyanide; a woman paralyzed,

her thoughts strobe-flashing as her body calcifies.
Rescued, his eyes search for the cranes—squealing,
framed in soap-dish blue. When he says *Reek!*
maybe he means *Spider, kiss me.* Maybe
he means *I miss you, Mother Sky.*

One Story

It starts in Philly, where the maternity nurse loves Connie Mack's
Athletics, who usually lose and will soon move to Kansas City
without the carrot-topped shortstop who gives C his nickname.
Or it starts on a Maryland dairy farm, where mornings smell
like flapjacks and manure, sausage and hay—where, of six
children, one dies of scarlet fever, one of whooping cough,
while three brothers and C's mother survive. Or it starts in New
Zealand: A boy, fourteen, ships out as a deckhand on a steamer
bound for London, where in three years, he'll meet his future wife.

Agamemnon, a box turtle, is in the story—and a turtle named
Inspector because he cranes his head to stare at C, and one named
Goof-Off because he bites, and one named Churchy after the turtle
in the comic strip C's mother reads to him. One day the thunder
sounds like God is pounding on the hull of a huge battleship.
One day the wind sounds like a python sliding through the trees.
A rock-and-roll band is involved, a smart kid—scorned by the Cool
Dudes—crowned overnight as the curtain rises on him, gripping
a red Gibson guitar, hamfisting through Freddie King's "San José."

Sometimes birdsongs outside C's room sound like creek songs
winding through pasture, then scarlet maple trees. Look closely
and you'll see pill bugs bustling beside a wood-frame house,
a bristly wolf spider squeezing under the door, about to toggle
C's mother to scream, punching the button marked *Arachnophobia*
in her son's brain. The story has the swirl and turmoil
of van Gogh, the thrust and drive of Beethoven, the palette
of Matisse—cherry, coral, plum, indigo, saffron, amber,
lime, jade—though C will call them red, blue, yellow, green.

Highlights include a week's fishing outside Kamloops, three-
for-four with a home run that wins the Oaks Dads Club pennant,
a divorce urged by a bitter therapist, a wedding interrupted
when a helicopter crashes in orange flames on the church lawn.
There are many love scenes—some better than others—
several loves, some of them "true." The story ends in a hospital:
an explosion of blood as C's son, daughter, and wife sob.
The story ends in a nursing home when C's ninety-year-old heart
mercifully stops. The story ends in Moorea, tenth anniversary

of C's second wedding: riptide, panic, unconscious
drifting, sea-mouths wearing him away. The story ends—
its best parts still unconceived—with an engine roaring up a hill,
the author putting down his pen, rushing to trundle out his big
green garbage can to meet the fuming, beetle-browed black truck
twenty years before Agamemnon, who scaled C's chicken-wire
turtle pen during a summer thunderstorm, and lived in a vacant lot
for years, is found by another red-haired boy, dropped
into White Oak Bayou, and floats all the way to Galveston.

Umbrellas

Miles of yellow parachutes-on-sticks,
pencil-necked mushrooms, buttercups
blown inside out—all popping up
on the curved arm of Highway 5.
The same thing, in blue, erupting in Japan

on the same day, like bilateral boils.
But prettier. It's art. The artist—Christo?
Cristo? Crisco?—pumped in six million
of his own dollars, cash. Twice
that many people came to gasp and stare.

Cars flowed up and down the 5
like colored bubbles in an IV tube.
"A triumph!" the *Times* declared.
Then wind sucked one umbrella up
and blowgunned it across the road.

Speared a spectator in the chest.
Made front-page news. Now
the artist's pulling his umbrellas down.
Poor guy's depressed. He can't go on.
As if people don't die more ignominiously

every day: A paper cut turns gangrenous.
A vat of molten lipstick dumps
on someone's head. No telling what
conch shell may hold a black widow
poised to whisper, "Poof, you're dead."

Stand with me, my beauty, in the wind.
Let us think of art, and blood tests
before marriage, and how love may come,
at any instant, flying through the air
to pierce our neck or skull or lungs or heart.

Broken Toe

Blessings on you, toe of many colors:
purple as a grape, maroon as a raspberry,
yellow as a ripe casaba, greenish-white as honey-
dew where the doctor's adhesive pressed.

I've been boring lately, puffy little pig.
I've complained, "Nothing ever happens to me,"
swollen bread stick, stumpy penis gorged
with blood. I was sunk in complacency

with my good salary, good job, good girlfriend,
writing good poems about nothing (or next to)
not to offend the eight or ten good people
who read them. "Goddamn it fuck shit cocksucker

O Judas hump!"—it was a prayer you pulled from me,
fat gouty priest, when, in the dark, I tripped
on my Heater-Plus-Fan. "Motherfucking asshole
goddamn slutty shit-face, fuck fuck fuck!"

A word-orgasm after long celibacy. Blessed release!
How did I stand the unfractured monotony?
Welcome back, pain. Welcome back, passion.
Welcome back, something-to-howl-about,

grist for the *How're-you-doing?* mill. Remind me
of the joys of walking, jump rope, running,
playing footsie. Hammer home the certainty
of decay, memento mori at my body's end.

In the TV screen of your bruised nail, I see the usual
skulls and skeletons, but also wheelchairs,
triple-bypass surgeries, hit-and-runs,
cancers, deaths by earthquake, flood, and killer bee.

The words *fragility* and *tenuous* flow by
like banners towed by blimps. I wasn't drunk.
I kicked no woman, dog, or door, though if you like
to think I did, dear reader, do. Believe I broke

my toe drop-kicking ninjas, if it pleases you.
Simply to reach the fridge is an adventure.
I hop on one leg to answer the phone.
It took ten minutes, the first day, to get my shoe on.

When I found that I could not depress my clutch
and had to give up my day's plans,
I swore a good two minutes more, then hopped
inside, crimson with rage and pride—

with real conflict in my life—
with an ache so sharp that when I stepped
I cried "Jesus!"—with my heart's silence broken—
with something to say.

Peaches

was her name—this fat lady who lived three houses down.
She wore big flowery nightgowns, and a polka-dot scarf
around her head like that black lady on the pancake mix.
She held her face hard and tight, like it was packed with so much lard,
if she relaxed, it would've dripped like candle wax. She had a boy

named Elwin—albino, deaf and dumb and blind, eyes sunk
back in his head like marbles, rolling up. He pranced
when he ran, like a puppet on strings. He'd smash into things
and fall, but not as often as you'd think. He worked his way
into strange places—our shed out back, or underneath the sink;

it was all blackness to him. He cost me a year's growth,
Mom said, the day I found him in my closet like some drooling
ghost. I knew I'd rather die than live like him.
"He'll get run over for sure," all the moms said. They'd clump
in our front yard, whispered words like *White trash*,

Welfare baby, *It ain't right*, leaping like sparks into my ears.
I was forbidden to play in Peaches' yard, or ask
her for a trick-or-treat, but one day I had Cub Scout candy
to sell. She looked as if she liked to eat . . .
I went to knock, then heard moaning from her window.

"O God," Peaches groaned, "O Jesus Lord . . ."
She was naked on her back in bed, fat titties hanging down
on either side, and Elwin's head in the thick moss that curled
and crackled between her hippo thighs. I couldn't tell what
he was doing, but I watched until she saw me, yanked him up,

and held him like a shield across her chest. "What you doin' here?"
she screamed. "Nothin'," I said, wanting to run. Her stare
froze me. "You think you're somethin', don't you, boy?"
"No ma'am," I lied. "Look at you," she snarled, so fierce I checked
to see my pants were zipped. "You've got your mom and dad

and that red two-wheeler with them trainin' wheels. Alls I got
is Elwin. All he's got is me. You get him took away, God'll take
somethin' from you, wait and see." That unfroze me. I shagged
for home like I'd been blasted by hellfire. But as cicadas tuned up
for the night, their buzzes gusting through the trees, and I tried

to think what I should tell my mom, something rose out of my head,
surrounding me with heat and light like angels in the Bible do.
Maybe I was scared that I'd get spanked for trespassing
in Peaches' yard, or that I'd say bad words explaining
what I'd seen, or maybe I didn't want to risk God taking my new

Huffy bike from me; but in that glow behind my eyes, I saw
how Peaches lay in bed, her moon face smiling and glad,
how Elwin clung to her like a monkey baby at the zoo,
and even after Peaches got cancer, and she and Elwin moved
away, I never told until now what I saw that day.

Invocation to Allen as the Muse Euterpe

Rise up, Allen, and appear to me.
Wherever you are, with whatever muscled acolyte, appear barefoot,
    in flowing robes, playing your flute, lilacs and orchids in your hair.
Or come as Erato if you prefer, or Polyhymnia, or Orpheus's mom,
    Calliope.
Prance in leading a circus, if it pleases you.
Or walk in, professorial and dignified: asp the Establishment took to its
    heart.

Scream through a microphone, or whisper in my ear (no tongue, Al,
    please).
Come from the fifties, your best years, reeking of reefer and whiskey,
    gism and sweaty underwear.
Come help me celebrate my failings, to admit how much it hurts to be
    barely five-seven—I who dreamed of being six-foot-three.
Come with Carl Solomon, Bill Burroughs, Herbert Huncke-rhymes-
    with-junkie, who robbed you blind to feed his habit, got you jailed
    as a burglar—but you took him back.

Come from Columbia, freshly expelled.
Come with your mother, Naomi, whom you committed to Pilgrim State
    Hospital—who thought her husband and your *buba* were conspiring
    with Franco, Hitler, Roosevelt to kill her—whose lobotomy you
    authorized—whose funeral, which you did not attend, lacked enough
    males to have a Kaddish read, so that later you wrote "Kaddish" for her.
Help me admit that I abandoned my parents when they got too sick and
    old and floated out of their right minds—that I dumped them—Dad,
    then Mom—on my sister, and blamed my strenuous schedule, my
    happening life: teaching, doing therapy, re-marrying, and of course
    writing poetry.

Help me admit how totally I've failed at that: in my fifth decade, without
a major book.

Come, sweet sunflower, trailing your addicts and addictions.
Come sick with love for Neal and Jack.
Come rattling the *Playboy* interview where you sang the joys of
buggery.
Give me machinegun bebop words, peyote psilocybin Nembutal jazz
words to immortalize the way I cheated on my wife, made her
hate her goodness and solidity by proving they weren't enough
for me.

Help me express my shame, my greed, my pettiness—the one grand
thing about me.
Don't stop there. Help me quit griping and celebrate L.A.: its corpse-
blue sky,
its Bel air and Beverly hills, its gurus and gangbangers, beaches and
waves into which, diving, you taste seven million bowels.
Help me to surface beaming, a turd-crown in my hair.
You who could love cold-water flats, cockroaches and bedbugs (human
and otherwise), come with your minor poet father, your slipshod
Buddhism, and "first word, best word" certainty.

Help me to sing of Hollywood pushers and peep shows and aging stars
ground underfoot, of Angelyne, "famous for nothing," who looks
down like God on rush hour with her abuse-me eyes above her
continental chest's white divide.
Appear to me, Allen, railing against Moloch in anticapitalist frenzy,
fresh from hallucinogenic quests to Mexico and Amazon, trailing
visions of Whitman, Blake, and Piggly Wiggly West.
Help me to be more than just me.
Help me admit in raving holy poetry that I protested Vietnam not
because of my high morals; because I was scared to go—

That I'm scared most of the time—that I lift weights and kickbox trying
    to be less scared—
That when I had a prostate biopsy, I whined like a baby, and when
    the needle bit, called the doctor a dickface, the nurse a whore.
Help me confess the whole fiasco with Carol Drake, how tenuous
    my potency can be, how much ass I've kissed in my life, how many
    miles of shit I've wolfed, how eagerly.
You owe me, Allen—I bought your biography. No, actually I was too
    cheap. My cousin in publishing sent it to me free. (A cousin in
    publishing, and still no book!)

I have no magnanimity of spirit. I don't want to embrace all human-
    kind. I don't like bad breath and BO. I don't like scabies and TB.
    I especially don't like embracing men. Oh, I can do it—the hard
    bear hug, the forced heartiness—I'm an L.A. shrink! But men
    feel so clunky and thick, clutching each other like bad dancers
    afraid to start waltzing around the room.
All so we won't look homophobic.
Come to me, Allen; I'm not afraid of you.
I know I have no breadth of vision and no depth. I know I lack heart.
    Give me a transplant. Please.
The instant I saw you in your white pajamas, 1970, thumbnailing your
    harmonium, braying in your love-fest hippie-beaded tuneless voice,
    leaping around, an awkward, shameless spaz, chanting and
    dancing, ecstatic, orgiastic, delighted, joyous, gleeful, gladsome,
    gay—really, truly gay—telling a thousand college kids about your
    lips against a black policeman's chest, begging "Please Master,"
    encanting "Please Master," praising God "Please Master," I knew
    if you could face the world that way, with your pubic beard, bald
    rabbi's head, hideous black glasses, and bare, pudgy, queer soul,
    then anything was possible, even for me.

The Shape of History

Turning and turning in the widening gyre . . .

Today's paper is crammed full of news: pages and pages on the Somalia Famine,
the Balkan Wars, Gays in the Military. On this date a year ago, only 1/365
of "The Year's Top Stories" happened. *Time Magazine* fits a decade into one
thin retrospective. Barely enough occurred a century ago to fill one
sub-chapter in a high school text. 500 years ago, one or two things
happened every 50 years. 5000 years ago, a city was founded,
a grain cultivated, a civilization toppled every other century.
Still farther back, the years march by in groups like grad-
uates at a big state university: 10,000 to 20,000 BC;
50,000 to 100,000 BC; 1 to 10 million BC. Before
that, things happened once an era: mammals in
the Cenozoic, dinosaurs in the Mesozoic,
forests in the Paleozoic, protozoans in
the Precambrian. Below that, at the
very base of time's twisting gyre,
its cornucopia, its ram's-horn
trumpet, its tornado tracking
across eternity, came what
Christians call Creation,
astrophysicists call the
Big Bang. Then, for
trillions of years,
nothing at
all.

from *Liver*   1999

Wedding Dress

She wants it and she doesn't want it: the lace neck
and sleeves, the waist so tight she'll need it re-fitted
the day before *the* day. She wants and doesn't want
the pleats and puffs and bows, the veil's force field
guarding her face, the train's long barge dragging behind,
the whole creation so elaborate she must be lowered
into it—like a knight onto his horse—with a crane.

She wants and doesn't want to choose her neckline:
bertha, bateau, jewel, Queen Anne, décolletage;
her sleeves: *bishop, balloon, pouf, gauntlet, mutton leg;*
her silhouette: *ballgown, basque, empire, sheath, mermaid;*
her headpiece: *pillbox, derby, wreath, tiara, garden hat.*
She wants and doesn't want the four-page guest list,
the country club that overlooks the valley

like a war party, eager to attack.
She wants and doesn't want the triptych invitations,
the florist/psychic who intones, "I envision one black
vase per table, each holding a single white rose."
"I love him," she thinks, "but my Zeppelin tapes are melting;
my Bowie posters curling into flame. I love him,
but Uni High is vanishing like our senior *Brigadoon.*

I love him but my friends are turning into toasters,
china place settings, crystal salad bowls."
She wants and doesn't want the plane door closing,
Tahiti rushing toward her, then dropping behind,
Mom in her fuchsia gown starting to stoop,
Dad giving her away as white hair falls: a fairy ring
around his feet. Even as she pays for it, her dress

is yellowing, the wedding pictures aging into artifacts,
her children staring at strangers: one in a penguin suit,
one in her glory. They can't believe that living
works this way—just as the boy can't believe what else
his pecker will be for; the girl, where babies grow,
how they get there, what every month will leak from her.
"I want it, but I don't want it," she'll say.

Over the Town

Chagall looks thrilled to be sporting his best green shirt,
holding his wife, Bella, in the cross-chest carry as they swim
above the red, green, and gray Russian town, Vitebsk.
I held Connie, my first girlfriend, that way as we practiced life-

saving in the class where we met, both of us fifteen. Come fall,
she dumped me for a senior; still, while they lasted, our days
seemed to float, changeless as stars in the June sky (though physics
swore the stars were rocketing away). While other artists mope,

look how happy Chagall is to be, in *Birthday*, an armless,
flying worm-man—a green-shirted, floating eel-man twisting
around from behind to kiss Bella, who holds a red, yellow, blue,
and white bouquet. He painted *Birthday* after Bella visited

on his, and made him feel above paltry physical laws.
Unthinkable not to be able to float, at any time, to Bella's lips.
Inconceivable that in 1944, "unexpectedly," the museum notes say
(how could a man in love ever expect such catastrophe?),

Bella would die, and change love's timeless present to the past
that people mourn, not comprehending how happiness solid
as a mountain could just blip away. Years in the future, today
will be part of my Golden Age. And yesterday, with its hot

blueberry bagels, its kissing on the couch as we watched
Cemetery Man. I swear I'll never let us lump into "the past,"
the way my years at home have bunched into "when I was a boy"
events separate and brilliant as the stars above pre-smog Houston:

the same stars Chagall and Bella loved over Vitebsk.
Standing in the very room where a painter named Gerbil
threw up cherry Jell-O to protest art's sterility, I pick your pink-
and-blue-flowered dress out of the crowd, walk up behind you,

smooth your chestnut hair, then lean around (feet stuck like magnets
to the floor) and kiss you. I fold my arms around you in the cross-
chest carry, and mentally at least, lift you as if to float forever
high over L.A. As if I, mortal myself, could save your life.

Biblical Also-Rans

Hanoch, Pallu, Hezron, Carmi,
Jemuel, Ohad, Zohar, Shuni:
one Genesis mention's all you got.

Ziphion, Muppim, Arodi: lost
in a list even the most devout skip over
like small towns on the road to L.A.

How tall were you, Shillim?
What was your favorite color, Ard?
Did you love your wife, Iob?

Not even her name survives.
Adam, Eve, Abel, Cain—
these are the stars crowds surge to see.

Each hour thousands of Josephs,
Jacobs, Benjamins are born.
How many Oholibamahs? How many

Mizzahs draw first breath today?
Gatam, Kenaz, Reuel? Side-men
in the band. Waiters who bring

the Pérignon and disappear.
Yet they loved dawn's garnet light
as much as Moses did. They drank

wine with as much delight.
I thought my life would line me up
with Samuel, Isaac, Joshua.

Instead I stand with Basemath, Hoglah,
Ammihud. Theirs are the names
I honor; theirs, the deaths I feel,

their children's tears loud as any
on the corpse of Abraham, their smiles
as missed, the earth as desolate

without them: Pebbles on a hill.
Crumbs carried off by ants.
Jeush. Dishan. Nahath. Shammah.

Musk Turtle

While his relative the red-eared slider,
Trachemys scripta elegans, glides gracefully,
or darts, green-and-yellow legs a blur,

he humps across slimed bottom gravel—
bonsai hippo; unwitting clown of the aquarium.
Even his name is ignominy:

Sternotherus odoratus, "stinkpot musk."
A living id, he mounts male red-ears twice
his size, and clings—dwarf bronco rider;

Old Man of the Sea. At feeding time,
the red-ears splash and bully, webbed feet
in his face, shoving him down. He paws the water

like a drowning man, lacking the spirit
to seize a gracile neck or elegant
striped leg in his knife-jaws. The rare times

he breaks through the mob, he can't catch
bloodworm pellets as they do. His mouth gapes:
a clumsy fielder's glove. He lunges,

drops the ball, then sinks to the bottom to skulk,
and scavenge what slips by. None of his kind
will ever crawl through steaming forests

after rain, feasting on dewberries and soft
grubs like the box turtle, or glide through bluegreen
waters over coral like the hawksbill,

or squat like the alligator snapper underneath
a rotten stump, ready to slice
some silver darter, drag some blithe duckling

down. Yet when beautiful things die—
the frilly koi, the leopard frog, the black-
spotted newt, the red-eared slider—it's the musk

turtle who cleans the mess their beauties leave—
whose wide mouth opens to accept, whose tongue,
shaped like a soft, pink heart, enfolds them all.

Tone of Voice

It pinks the cheeks of speech, or flushes the forehead.
It's a spring breeze in which words play, a scorching sun

that burns them red, slate clouds that cover them in ice.
Mastering tone, the child outgrows his sticks and stones.

"Okay," he sneers, twisting the word in Mommy's eye.
Ellipses, dashes, underlines, ALL CAPS are clumsy

tuna nets through which tone's minnows slide.
"I love you" may arrive spiked like a mace, or snickering.

"State your name," from lawyers' lips, can mean "You lie!"
Tone leaks the truth despite our best efforts to hide.

It's verbal garlic; mistress on a husband's hands.
Consider, dear, when you ask, "Where are my French fries?"

how you may stand in a silk teddy holding grapes,
a suit of mail holding a lance, a hangman's hood holding

a rope. As useless to protest, "I didn't mean that,"
as to tell a corpse, "Stand up. You misinterpreted my car."

Tenderness in Men

It's like plum custard at the heart of a steel girder,
cool malted milk in a hot bowling ball.

It's glimpsed sometimes when a man pats a puppy.
If his wife moves softly, it may flutter like a hermit thrush

into the bedroom, and pipe its pure, warbling tune.
Comment, though, and it's a moray jerking back into its cave.

Dad taught me to hide tenderness like my "tallywhacker"—
not to want or accept it from other men. All I can do

for a friend in agony is turn my eyes and, pretending
to clap him on the back, brace up his carapace with mine.

So, when you lean across the table and extend your hand,
your brown eyes wanting only good for me, it's no wonder

my own eyes glow and swell too big for their sockets
as, in my brain, dry gulleys start to flow.

Prozac

It's transforming the world the way Leary said dropping acid,
Maharishi said meditation, Christ said Christianity would.
Polly next door, bedridden since her husband's stroke,

laughs from her car, "It makes me tipsy, like champagne."
Clients in psychotherapy, after sweating years like miners
in the bowels of the unconscious, gulp their tabs and say they're cured.

Cartoons appear: Poe tells a raven, "Nice birdie."
Hitler, dancing the hora, shouts, "Master race, schmaster race."
Patrick Henry proclaims, "Give me liberty, or twenty milligrams."

Friends slide into the fold. My ex-wife calls to say, "I can't believe it—
I see things your way!" This is more radical than microchips,
cloning, genetic engineering, virtual reality. Aggressor nations

may fall to Prozac bombs. Many will die, but few will care.
To mourn will seem as strange as wishing people still shrieked
through surgeries, made pumpernickel loaves from scratch,

dragged covered wagons over prairies full of Indians,
just to own a home. Teenagers, to rebel, will refuse drugs.
They'll return from dates at nine o'clock—still virgins—and scream

at their parents, who sprawl, munching nachos and giggling
at car crashes, in front of the boob tube. They'll run to their rooms
in despair, finish their homework, then write of their discovery

of pain. It gives such depth to life, they'll say, such swirls
of nuance: crimson, purple, emerald, pink. If everyone could feel
this way, they think, it would transform the world.

Byron, Keats, and Shelley

Decide to temper Romantic *Sturm und Drang* with comedy.
    Keats shaves his head;
        Shelley frizzes out his hair;
Byron submits to a bowl cut.

    My heart aches, and a drowsy numbness pains
        My sense, as though of hemlock I had drunk,
Keats sighs, his head stuck in a cannon.

    Eternal Spirit of the chainless Mind!
        Brightest in dungeons, Liberty!
Byron shouts, and lights the fuse.

O wild West Wind, thou breath of Autumn's being,
    Thou, from whose unseen presence the leaves dead
        Are driven, like ghosts from an enchanter fleeing,
Shelley booms, and drops a cannonball on Byron's toe.

    Exiled to the continent, they write their famous
        Trilogy: *Idiots Deluxe, Half-Wit's Holiday,*
And their masterpiece, *Mummies Dummies,*

    In which Byron plays Ozymandias embalmed,
        And Keats gets his nose slammed in a sarcophagus,
Runs face-first into a sphinx, and staggers

Around rubbing his pate as Shelley mugs beside
    The shattered sphinx and states, *Round the decay*
        Of that colossal wreck, boundless and bare,
The lone and level sands stretch far away . . .

Then the curtain falls on his chin.
        The trio tour Paris, Berlin, Vienna, Prague—
Tuba players blowing wigs off heads of state;

        Dogcatchers wrapped in their own nets;
           Waiters flinging cream pies,
Dumping cauldrons of hot soup in courtly laps

Until they die, too young, careening
        Into immortality covered with flour, squealing,
           Drainpipes on their heads—which explains why
For many years, the greatest poems

        In English have all ended *Nyuk, nyuk, nyuk,*
           And why, reading *She walks in beauty like the night* . . .
We are as clouds that veil the midnight moon . . .

        Season of mist and mellow fruitfulness . . .
        You may feel ghostly pliers tweak your nose,
And ghostly fingers poke the tear ducts in both eyes.

Someone Else's Good News

Even as I say, "That's fantastic!
I'm glad for you," my hand quivers, my mood
Conks out, flaming, at thirty thousand feet.
What is the sound of "overjoyed," and how
Convey it, as if what is good for friends
Is good for me—as if my own crippled
Hopes aren't leaping off gurneys, flopping
Out of wheelchairs screaming, "Shit! Shit! Why
Wasn't it me?!" Sheepish good sport, bloody-
Nosed loser shaking the champion's hand,
Poor jilted chump who sends a wedding gift
And sings "Take good care of my baby,"
I wince to hear how winner Joan almost
Skipped the contest I've entered faithfully
For twenty years, how winner John rang
The wrong doorbell and blundered into the woman
I've spent thousands on dating services
And flirting seminars trying to find.
I feel mean, treacherous, small, fighting
Not to think "Get cancer," "Die in a car wreck,"
"Be burned alive with your pisshead cheerful
Wife and noisy, overindulged kids."
Trophy trout leaping on every line
But mine, I crash upstream, downstream, cursed
By everyone whose cast I cross, whose hole
I hog. All dignity lost, all pretense gone,
I foam like an envy-salted snail.
Acid in my eyes: the excitement
Of the fortunate, the grin (politely restrained)
That says I've done it! I've arrived!

While for me it's *Oh God no*, back
To page one, back to the empty canvas, back
To the old job, back to the hands above
The keyboard, paralyzed, not knowing how
To start again. I wave as friends' yachts leave
The dock, straining to hoist the corners
Of my mouth, although the little Atlases
Supporting them have gulped bad oysters, and
Just want to lie down, just want to throw up.

Losing My Hair

How can I walk outside without its springs
to bounce the sun back from my face?
How can I take my blind mother to church
and be seen as her life's potent continuation
if hair stops doing copper pushups on my head?

How can I survive beautiful girls' eyes
with no curls crackling, "I'm full of fire for you!"
How can I not, at work, seem foolish, middle-
aged (must middle age always seem foolish?)
if no Birds of Promise nest above my brain?

Soft roof of the body's mansion—sleek
fur hat—pine-needled carpet covering
my bright ideas—protein extrusions,
helping me build happy times—
how can I order a Big Mac and feel kin

to the checkout girl, and not the dour drudge
with his name tag: "Hank Skelley, Manager"?
How can I start my car with a boyish
wrist flick? How can I fly coach class
to Denver, not mistaken for a mortal

who, if his plane crashed, could die?
Bring me potions, grafts, weavings, wigs,
gene therapy! How else can I get back
my seat in seventh grade? How else can I
hunt Easter eggs, rejoin the Peewee League,

claim my half-price movie tickets,
my child's plate? Crown, miter, headdress
of youthful office, what should I do?
My head's a planet with failing gravity.
One by one its people fall into the sky.

Love Poetry

Most people think it's what all poetry is—
that, or incomprehensible, which love is too.
But wonderful. Enough to make you swim
the Hellespont—or try. Enough to make
you drink poison, or shoot yourself to warn
your lover of a trap. Forget the cynics
who call you "codependent." What do they know
about love? It's better than being president.
Better than discovering a cure for death,
your face on stamps from every country
in the world. Better than eating anything
you want and not gaining an ounce—
getting more physically fit with every Devilish
Mocha Cheesecake Delight. Look at pop songs,
movies, books—so many people burning
calories in love's praise. Don't tell me
they "protest too much." All cynics are casualties
of love. They start hopeful as anyone,
but instead of strawberry crepes on Sunday morning,
they get a spider sandwich. Instead of hot oil
massages, they get drubbed with baseball bats.
Instead of all-expense-paid lives in Bora Bora,
they get the Gulag Archipelago.
                                        Forget them.
See that couple ditching school? See how
she grips his arm at the elbow? See how they stop
on the sidewalk in front of the whole passing
adult world, and kiss? *French* kiss! See how
he kneads her ass?—not only without shame,
with pride. Look how proud they are of each other

as they resume walking, love tinting the air
around them like a big red heart. That isn't pap;
that's poetry. Even if she gets pregnant today,
and wrecks her life. Even if her father makes her
abort the child and dump the guy. Even if
he finds a new girlfriend and flaunts her,
while his dream to be a rock star shrinks to a vow
to fish a lot, then dwindles to dust under his bed.
Even if she marries a cop who beats her,
and punches three kids into her before she's twenty.
Even if the boy—now more or less a man—
sees her one day shopping at Ralph's, and doesn't
know her, she looks so sad and old. Even if
that girl was you, that boy was me. Even so.

Descent

for Erik

Let
there be
amino acids,
and there were: a slop
of molecules in ancient seas,
building cell walls to preserve their
identities, dividing, replicating, starting
to diversify, one growing oars, one rotors, one
a wiry tail, lumping into clusters—cyanobacteria, sea
worms, medusae, trilobites, lobe-finned fish dragging onto
land, becoming thrinaxodon, protoceratops, growing larger—
diplodocus, gorgosaurus—dying out—apatosaurus, tyrannosaurus—
mammals evolving from shrew-like deltatheridium into hyenadon, eohippus,
mammoth, saber-tooth, dire wolf, australopithecus rising on two feet, homo erectus
tramping from Africa into Europe and Asia, thriving like a weed that will grow anywhere—
jungle, desert, snow-pack—the genetic rivers flowing downhill now: a husband's skull crushed
in the Alps, a Tartar raping a green-eyed girl who dies in childbirth, whose daughter falls in
love with a Viking who takes her to Istanbul, a Celt who marries a Saxon, a weaver
who abducts the daughter of a witch, a son who steals his father's gold, a girl
who loses one eye leaping from a tree, dozens who die of smallpox,
cholera, black plague, a knight, a prostitute, thieves, carpenters,
farmers, poachers, blacksmiths, seamstresses, peddlers of
odds and ends, an Irishman who sells his family into
servitude, a Limey who jumps ship in New York,
Jews who flee Hungary, a midwife, an X-ray
machine repairman, a psychologist,
a writer, all flowing down,
converging on the great
delta, the point
of all this:
you.

from *Tulip Farms and Leper Colonies*   2001

Did That Really Happen?

Asked after readings

Do I ask you, reader, if that's your own hair?
If those are your real breasts? If that fat is natural,
or you had it pumped in to fend off what otherwise
would be unbearable celebrity? What if,

like the president, I "don't recall"? Memory's
a wisp of thread, a broken hair about to fall,
a dandelion seed in a breeze, a blob of oil in water,
changing constantly. Did my Cub Scout den mother

pull her panties down, and make me "kiss the kitty"?
Yes, if wishing counts. (Haven't you dreamed
someone loved you, and wakened, certain it was true?)
We know embarrassment erases memory;

look what it did after Mom found you modeling
her bra, whispering "Boo, bees!" I admit
I stole my best friend's girl in seventh grade.
But I didn't get her pregnant, as I've claimed in print.

She didn't give birth to a hairball with eight eyes.
(Though could I really make that up out of blue sky?)
Maybe that daycare worker did kill elephants,
and make kids foo-woo on one another's heads.

Maybe Satan did rear out of the sandbox to gulp babies.
Maybe Manassas and Agincourt were tulip farms,
or leper colonies, or old ladies who made lederhosen
and the world's most lethal bean soufflé.

Ten years ago the *Times* blistered my book.
I doctored the review, then used revised "quotes"
in my résumé. A week ago, a reporter
read the résumé; today, the *Times* quotes me.

Cornflowers sway outside my window, pink
and blue. Orange milkworts pogo in the breeze.
Or did I see them in a coffee table book?
What's the difference? Now they belong to you.

To Prove that We Existed Before You Were Born,

we'll tell you how your mom worked at the hospital,
treating people like the tattered, gray-faced man
who shoves his shopping cart down Verdugo,
muttering to the czar. How, between bouts
at my desk, I'd bumble barefoot through the house,
feeding our fish, or patting Marvin, the cat.

Mom will tell how, at her first job, age sixteen,
she found a dead mouse in Baskin-Robbins' hot fudge,
called the manager at home, and when he didn't
believe her, dropped the chocolate-covered Mickey
on his big desk blotter, and never returned.
I'll resurrect my sunburst Stratocaster from its coffin-

case, and show how I played at The Catacombs,
and clubbed a Bandido who rushed the stage.
I might even tell how, my red pickup sagging
with band gear, I'd pull away from girlfriends
in Portland, Billings, Coeur d'Alene, and barely see
the road for tears until, in a few miles,

the clouds lifted, a surge of freedom picked me up,
and, surfing on its crest, I'd start to sing.
You'll smile as if you're hearing *Jack the Giant-Killer*
and *Snow White*—as if our lives are fairy tales
from olden days. Your world will be about your
friends, your baseball, your Tickle Me Elmo,

or whatever the fad is. You won't care that the musk
of narcissus on a March day made us feel sexy,

just as it will you. You'd never guess
that, when you were a neural tube, an ember
trying to make a flame, your mom felt sick,
so we went walking on the street we were leaving

to find a better place for you. A north wind
gnawed our lips, but as we walked, holding hands
inside my parka pocket, your mom's nausea lifted,
as did my grief to feel you stealing her from me.
Inventing songs about our turtles—Mr. Cow,
Peg Webb, Trout-Boy, and Tammy Faye—

we started laughing, and stopped on the sidewalk
(cracked by the last earthquake), and kissed
as long and desperately as if we were saying goodbye—
kissed the way our parents may have
(since we're both eldest children)—kissed as if
we didn't need you, one last time.

Charles Harper Webb

"Manly," my mother said my first name meant.
I enjoyed sharing it with kings, but had nightmares
about black-hooded axmen lifting bloody heads.

I loved the concept of *Charlemagne*, and inked
it on my baseball glove and basketball.
I learned that females pronounce "Charles" easily;

males rebel. Their faces twitch, turn red as stutterers'.
Finally they spit out "Chuck" or "Charlie."
Charles is a butler's name, or a hairdresser's, they explain.

(I'll bet Charles Manson would straighten
those guys' tails. I'll bet he'd fix their hair just right.)
My name contains its own plural, its own possessive.

Unlike Bob or Bill or Jim, it won't just rhyme with anything.
I told Miss Pratt, my eighth-grade French teacher,
"*Charles* sounds like a wimp." I switched to German to be *Karl*.

Of all possible speech, I hear "Charles" best.
I pluck it from a sea of noise the way an osprey plucks a fish.
In print, it leaps out before even sex words do.

My ears twitch, eager as a dog's. What sweet terror
in the sound: Is Charles there? Oh, *Charles*.
Oh, Charles. *Oh, Charles*. Charles, see me after class.

Get in this house, Charles Harper Webb!
Harper—nag, angel, medieval musician.
Webb, from Middle English *webbe*, weaver (as in the web

of my least favorite crawling thing), my pale ancestors
stoop-shouldered, with sneezing allergies,
stupefied by the loom's endless *clack clack clack*,

squatting in dirt-floored cottages year after year,
poking out every few decades to see armed men gallop past,
followed by the purple passage of a king.

Vikings

Overran my boyhood dreams—fierce
Blond beards, slab chests,
Biceps gripped by bronze bands,
Dragon ships which terrorized my ancestors,
Weak Britons who whined to Christ:

No match for Odin, or the hard hammer
Of Thor. While other kids clutched
Toy guns and grenades, I swung
My plastic war ax—immune to bullets,
Refusing to die. While they dreamed

Of rocketing through sunny skies,
I dreamed of fjords, their crags and storms
Matching my dark moods, my doubts
Of God, my rages and my ecstasies.
I snuck in twice to see *The Norseman*,

Wincing but bearing it as the Saxon king
Chopped off Prince Gunnar's right
Hand. I gloried in the sulking gods
And ravens and great trees, roots
Reaching underground to realms

Of dwarfs and trolls. I gloried in the runes
On shields, the long oar strokes
That sliced through ocean cold as steel.
I gloried in the Valkyries bearing slain
Heroes to the mead halls of Valhalla

To feast and fight and fondle blonde
Beauties forever, while we sad
Methodists plucked harps and fluttered:
Sissies Mommy had to dress
For Sunday school. The day before

Christmas vacation, when Danny Flynn
Called me "a fish-lipped fool,"
I grabbed a trashcan lid and slammed it
Like a war shield in his face. Then,
While teachers shrilled their whistles,

And Mr. Bean, the porky principal,
Scurried for his ax, I leapt over
Danny's blood and bawling, thrust
My sword-hand in my shirt, and stalked out
Into the cruel winter of third grade.

A Salesman and a Librarian

The rest are chastised and reborn
as salesmen and librarians.

From "Doing This," by Tony Hoagland

Mom smelled of books, even Dad admitted
between "prospects," as he called everyone.
In the checkout line at Vons, he'd show strangers
his coat, watch, pants, and say, "Make me an offer."
"Shh," Mom would tell him. "Honey, sshh."

When friends came over to play baseball, Dad
hawked peanuts. Mom made the umpire whisper.
All my parties were the slumber kind.
At least nobody stayed awake to watch
Mom catalog my clothes and toys, my cute

sayings and minuscule misdeeds. I loved
my parents, but prayed God would make them fun
like Joey's mom, whom people called "Madam,"
and Lynn's dad before the cops dragged him away.
Walking home from school, some days I'd miss

our house, it made such scant impression.
Or maybe I just couldn't bear to see Dad's car
always marked "For Sale," the lemonade stand
where he sat all night, the garage stuffed
with alphabetized newspapers and *Kirkus Reviews*

among unsold stain removers, *World Books*,
insurance policies. The vacuum cleaners especially
haunted me—too sad even to dust off
their bristly mustaches; too tired to raise,
on brontosaurus necks, their plastic hammer-heads.

Death Comes to the Baby Boom

Fire drills didn't get us ready, or bomb shelters,
     or *Dracula Has Risen from the Grave.*
         Not even
Vietnam prepared us for the ice cream truck

jingling "Stars and Stripes Forever" as Death waves
     pink Torpedos, exploding Eskimo
         Pies. Death comes
to us with a gray beard, leading a horse for picture-

taking. "Who is this clown—Gabby Hayes?" Bill quips,
     and feels a vein in his head blow. Death comes
         to us
as a new black-and-white TV. We watched Pinky

Lee clutch his chest and fall, gasping "Help me"
     to fifteen million kids. Still, we're amazed
         when Death—looking
like Howdy Doody, Phineas T. Bluster,

Princess Summer-Fall-Winter-Spring delivers milk
     laced with arsenic to our front door. Our friends
         scare us:
Clare's breasts, Harold's belly, Bobby's hair.

We dodge mirrors, skittish as vampires. Bad-thought
     alarm! Call 911 to report an Unsettling
         Thing! Death comes
as the *Gillette Fight of the Week.* Turn it on;

Sugar Ray's bony fist floors us; safety razors slit
        our jugulars. Death comes humming,
                "Brylcreem,
a little dab'll do ya." Death uses

Wild Root Cream Oil, Charlie. Death vows, "Someday,
        Alice—Pow! Right to the moon!" Death comes
                as a Dumbo
pen, blacking our teeth. Death comes as a brain-

eating Davy Crockett hat. Death comes as Elvis,
        crooning "Heart-Failure Hotel," "Hound Dog"
                ripping our throats,
hit 45s screaming like Dad's circular saw.

Death comes to us as a Mark Wilson Magic Set.
        Climb in the box; you won't climb out. Death comes
                as a black
hula hoop. Slip it over your head; you disappear.

Waking at 3 A.M.

Now is the time humans feel closest to the grave,
and ghosts, most nearly free from it.
We hear them creaking through the house,
see them sway with the shirts in our closet,

feel a chill as window shades lift in the wind
that slinks across our feet. Now is the time
when old wounds ache: the toe broken at hopscotch,
the thigh scarred in the game-losing slide.

Now the thoughts we've tried to hide
break free and tear us like harpies.
We're not good enough, and never will be.
The body's temperature is coldest now.

The heart beats slowest. Life sinks
to its lowest ebb. Time to give up.
Nothing's worth an effort, let alone a fight.
Failures slip into mind: tomb robbers,

stripping any dignity we've kept.
Time now for false epiphanies: *My life
would work if I could just play golf in church.*
I'll say I love my boss; that'll cinch a raise.

To wake now is to enter a locked room
where we've been warned never to go.
If we're alone, we recall the reasons why;
if coupled, we're long estranged.

We want to clutch the ones we've wronged,
and swear we'll change. But she is light-
years away; he's in another galaxy.
We want to think this is our man

snoring beside us, this our wife who sighs
and wraps more tightly in the comforter.
Try to touch him. I dare you.
                    Try to kiss her.

Cocksucker

I thought it was a myth, tied with *motherfucker*
for World's Most Disgusting Thing.
Just because some poor kid couldn't throw a ball,
or run, or talk without a lisp, didn't make him
a fairy, fruitcake, queen, queer, pansy, homo,
flaming fag—didn't mean he would do *that*.

My opinion made some say *I* must be one, and let me
practice the right cross–left hook Dad taught me.
When Sammy Blevins, Taft High's choir teacher,
got the spirit and proclaimed he'd been "an evil
sodomite till saved by Jesus' love" (Jesus Gonzales,
jokers sneered)—I admitted *cocksuckers* must be real.

Still, I had doubts until Del Delancey hired me
to play guitar for The Delmations, and we caught rainbow
trout and wrote neo-doowop and roomed together
on the road, and I had girls stay over, but he never did,
and when the band broke up, he said, "I love you, Chuck,"
and cried, certain I'd hate him. "It's hell," he said—

the hot iron boiling in his gut, the dark well
where, like that unkillable giant in *Grimm's Fairy Tales*,
he hid his heart. Remembering times I'd called some slow
driver or loudmouth drunk a cocksucker, I said,
"It's no big deal, Del." But I edged away.
"They do it up the Hershey highway like I like it,"

he wrote from Mexico—to punish me?—and he was gone,
folded and packed into the chest where I keep painful things

safe and out of sight. But then today I heard a joke
about a cork soaker, a Coke stocker, and a sock cutter.
When I told my wife, she said, "A good cocksucker's
what I pray to be."

Please, God, take care of Del.
Lead him safely through the long valley of AIDS.
Give him health, a hacienda, and a man
who worships him and does everything he likes.
Tell him for me—dream, telepathy, vision, it's up to You—
Del, my friend, you cocksucker, I loved you too.

Waiting

We sigh and fidget, waiting for the class to end.
We nod like therapists, and say "Uh-huh,"
waiting for the nagging to wind down, the battering
tongue to punch itself out. We curl in bed
waiting for our guts to calm, the chills and headaches

to subside. We can't stand the tension,
we decide, and smoke and drink and screw,
waiting to see if we get into Law School, bag
the Scholarship, drag home the Prize. Waiting
to marry and begin our lives. Waiting to know

if she's too hurt to stay, too in love to go. Waiting
for quitting time, for results of the biopsy, AIDS test,
licensing exam. Waiting for the proctologist
to withdraw, the nurse to suck out enough blood.
Oh hurry, hurry, we intone. Oh please, oh please.

Waiting for Sister to get out of the bathroom.
Waiting for our turn at bat; an autumn trout trip;
two weeks in Maui. Wondering if the earthquake's over,
or an 8.0 waits, cracking its knuckles in the dark.
Waiting to see if the cold sore heals before school pictures;

if our metatarsal mends, or we limp all our lives.
Waiting for the Picasso show, spring columbines,
summer vacation, fall duck hunting, snow and skis,
forgetting—Oh hurry, hurry. Please, oh please—
what horse we're spurring toward what finish line.

Socks

She thinks she's silly, making love in them.
"Sorry," she says. "My feet get cold."

She can't believe he loves the contrast—public
parts clothed, private not—the unsettling

quality, like clouds lolling on the ground
as rain falls up. Socks make her human—

no Maja in majesty, or Bunny with an airbrushed
muff. Socks show her frail and suffering,

a wounded thing, like Plato's people
when the gods cut male and female apart.

As a boy, he loved to give girls jewelry,
then pose them wearing just the silver necklace,

topaz earrings, turquoise brooch.
Now age has taught him all about cold feet.

He knows how small the range of temperature
that lets people live, how exacting their demands

of atmosphere. He knows how fragile
is that flesh people protect with cloth

and leather: tenderness on which they walk
or run or vault or hobble painfully

around the globe, forlorn as single socks
until they make a pair.

To Make My Countrymen Love Poetry

I wrote a priceless poem, a poem so precious
Burglars broke into my house three times
A day looking for it, and bankers begged
Me to deposit it with them, and women
Clamored for it instead of a ring,
And mafiosi clung like ants to the armored
Car I hired, and my own bodyguards mugged
And strip-searched, but didn't torture me
For fear I'd change one syllable.

I wrote an incriminating poem, a poem
So damning of so many that death threats
Arrived each hour; that police and FBI
Searched my house and car and safe-
Deposit box, with warrants and without,
Whether or not I was there, and attorneys
Begged to defend me just for the publicity,
And everyone I've ever known offered me
Big bucks to cut where they appeared.

I wrote an atomic poem, a poem
So devastating that the government
Begged to store it in a silo for me;
That one reading cured cancer, though
Memorizing it caused leukemia;
That traders in contraband offered missiles
Armed with warheads in exchange;
That no one who remembered even one line
Could stop shaking.

I wrote a Top Secret poem, a poem
So classified that not even the CIA
Knew of it (they'd heard rumors)—
A poem the president lacked clearance to see.
Every woman I slept with was a spy.
I couldn't eat a bowl of Raisin Bran without
Chipping molars on some flake-size *bug*.
The world's future lay in my hands,
And people listened when I said, *Don't startle me.*

I wrote a narcotic poem, a poem
So addictive that a single word,
Cut with a hundred neutral letters, sold
For thousands on the street; that junkies died
Of overdoses every day—died smiling,
Died fulfilled; that cocaine, heroin, speed,
Reefer, LSD lost all value;
That no one who heard so much as a prose
Summary could ever get enough.

I wrote a prophetic poem, a poem
So accurate that reporters used it
As a source; that racetracks, Lotto,
And all Nevada shut down; that elections
Were abolished—people just asked me
Who won. Religions sprang up around me.
People booked marriages, divorces,
Funerals years in advance, and no one
Lost a dime by listening to me.

I wrote an extraterrestrial poem, a poem
So advanced and powerful that lovers paused
Mid-kiss to hear; that lifelong enemies
Dropped their weapons and embraced; that no one

Passed within a mile of the text without
Choking up; that people stopped burning
Coal and gas and oil and wood, and gathered
Near the poem, and rubbed their numb hands,
And opened first their jackets, then their hearts.

from *Hot Popsicles*   2005

Consciousness

Satan drugged God's favorite pair of animals, and planted in their brains a shimmering seed.

At first, the seed glowed like the moon on cloudy nights. Then it flashed like the sky-fire that, even in hard rain, could make trees burn. Then it blazed like a second sun, coaxing the dark world out of hiding.

It made leaves greener, ponds wetter, dirt grittier, flowers and fruits so fragrant they seemed to yank all noses toward them.

"Who are you?" the two asked God the next time He walked in their garden.

"Stop staring," God said, and caused a wind to carry them into the desert while He wove fig leaves to hide His nakedness.

"You can come back," He called when He had finished. But they didn't come.

He found that He could see everything in the world except these two. He could know anything except their minds.

All night He called, "Come back to Eden." When, next morning, the famished pair left the cave where they'd been hiding, God saw, and brought them home.

But they didn't graze blissfully, or roll in thick grass as they'd done before.

"Your gut's too big," Eve told Adam.

God saw His own paunch, and winced.

"Don't climb that tree—you'll break your leg!" Adam told Eve, and God felt the fragility of His limbs.

"Sometimes I think you're adorable; other times, I want to slap you," Eve told Adam, and God realized he felt that way about Satan.

"Things seem good now," Adam told Eve one night after they made love. "But I can see us getting bored. I see you with flat, droopy breasts and a big rear. I see myself with gray hair spraying out my nose, and pain in both legs when I walk."

God scrambled back to heaven, but when He tried to sleep, He felt plaque choking off his arteries. He felt free radicals whiz through Him, His cells shattering like water jars.

When Adam's legs hurt too much to move, and Eve's heart fluttered, leaving her too weak to stand, God took no pleasure in their offspring, who carpeted the land. He felt frail as his favorites, realizing "I can't help them." Realizing—even worse—"They can't help Me."

Rat Defeated in a Landslide

When he's nominated, pundits are amazed. What were the party bosses thinking?

But Rat is confident. He knows where the country should go, and how to get there. He knows how to mark his territory with urine. His huge balls pendulate for all to see.

He campaigns well, at ease in gutter or chateau. He eats offal as easily as lobster quiche.

People hate his naked tail? No problem; he'll wear a mink sleeve.

"I'm a survivor," he says. Yet he is capable of as much sacrifice as his siblings, who died for research.

His biggest drawback is his name. "Don't trust that Rat," people warn. "What a Rat," they say.

Well, he can rise above such prejudice. His success will wash away all memory of plague and typhus, lice and fleas, chewed furniture, babies gnawed to death in cribs, nibbled wires causing conflagrations!

Our nation's floundering; Rat offers solid ground. Our nation's clueless; Rat has answers. Our nation's flailing aimlessly; Rat has a plan.

He makes a nest by shredding newspapers that predict his defeat. Election day, he votes early, then scurries back to his nest, and waits with his family for the returns.

Exit polls have him losing nine to one. "You could run a cockroach and get 10 percent," one commentator quips as state after state slips down Rat's opponent's hole.

The final vote: fifty to zip. The first shutout in U.S. history.

Rat congratulates his opponent, and graciously accepts the people's will.

Not so the bosses.

"You're finished, Rat," they rail, pluck him up by the neck, and drop him in a cage with the new candidate they're grooming: handsome, muscular, seven-foot-long Snake.

To Set Himself Off from the Crowd,

an individual pastes a gold skunk decal on his forehead.

Everyone he meets that day sports a gold skunk right between the eyes.

The individual broods all night, and drives to work next morning with a tortoise instead of a briefcase. But no mouths fall open. No one squeals, "How clever!" His co-workers go about their business, tortoise-briefcases under their arms.

The individual heads for the men's room to flush his tortoise. But it won't go down. The sewer lines are clogged with tortoises.

The individual fumes all day, works all night, then heads for the office next morning with his legs replaced by a steam-powered calliope that wheezes "Darktown Strutter's Ball." He arrives to find a horde of legless workmen-on-calliopes remodeling the building to accommodate the new "Locomotors," as they're being called when anyone can hear above the din of "Darktown Strutter's Ball."

"That's it, I quit! Let someone else feed the incredibly gross National Product!" the individual shouts. "I'm going home to get a suntan, have a hot, relaxing shower, and take a good book to bed."

At 10:05 a.m., he rolls out of his office into a sea of Locomotors: the worst traffic jam in history. The library, when he arrives, has been picked clean. It's past sundown when he chugs into his apartment to find a brown-out in progress, and barely enough water pressure for an ice-cold bath.

Conan the Barbarian

waited politely, in his best suit, for his turn to board the Greyhound, L.A.-bound. He picked two seats toward the rear, sprawled over both, and faked deep sleep.

Five minutes later, the bus eased into the rainy night with Conan sitting pretty: lots of legroom, and no neighbor to disrupt his reading practice.

Conan had gone civilized. He didn't miss Stygian ale. He didn't miss Red Sonja, or Belit, queen of the Black Coast. He liked his MasterCard, *The Tonight Show*, *Money Magazine*.

He switched on his reading light.

Nothing.

He switched on the light above his extra seat.

Still nothing.

All over the bus, happy people were switching on their reading lights, settling back to pass the long hours profitably, pleasurably, while he sat swathed in gloom.

There was not one other empty seat.

"Well, they can't blame me this time," Conan growled as he loosened his tie, stood, and reached into his golf bag for his sword.

A Ticklish Situation

Then there is the question: how to disrobe for swimming?

If a girl simply strips naked, she's immodest. If she takes off some clothes but leaves others on, she's still undressing, her motions sure to spawn lewd thoughts, the way a mother strolling with her child suggests nights of abandoned passion.

Is it better to arrive pre-dressed in a swimsuit, or to swim dressed in street clothes? Doesn't the one show too much skin, and the other show the strong desire *not* to show skin, which conjures visions of the most intimate skin?

And doesn't the failure to swim on a warm, sunny day suggest a wish to hide? And doesn't that imply feelings of guilt and shame, which bring to mind those body parts with which guilt and shame are linked?

There can be but one solution: to undress without undressing, swim without swimming, in the manner of one who, hearing sparrows chirp in the cherry tree outside her window, watches and enjoys them, while not hearing, watching, or enjoying them at all.

Judge Frosty Presiding

A man dressed in pajamas is arguing a case before a snowman. The lawyer (as he must be) speaks in a loud voice, striking what he hopes is a dramatic pose each time he makes an irrefutable point.

The judge sits in his black robes, melting.

The lawyer calls witnesses. But the one who takes the stand is never the one he called. So he calls a new witness, thinks of what he should have asked the old, and can't relocate him in the packed courtroom.

Now he insists that, with his knowledge of character, he can tell the judge exactly what each witness *would* have said. He gives examples, in the very words, with the very accents!

The judge keeps melting. His robes are soaked. His powdered wig has slipped over his eyes.

The lawyer argues louder. He's just realized that he is the defendant, too.

He pounds his fist on the huge books he keeps bringing "respectfully" to the court's attention. He refers to exhibits "A through double-D"—more and more inconsistent, praying no one notices, praying he can brass it out.

The judge keeps melting.

Only his top hat is visible above the bench. His corncob pipe, his coal eyes and teeth, have hit the floor. Now, gavel-like, his carrot nose begins to fall.

Imp of the Verbose

"Traffic's awful," says my colleague as we ride the elevator to our floor.

"It is," I say. "The only time I've seen it worse was the day my wife's mom died. We were due at the funeral home by noon, but I was having an affair, and couldn't pull myself away from my little sword-swallower. Once I did, I hit the traffic. When I finally made it home, my wife had overdosed on Xanax, and barfed all over our best Persian rug. Two thousand dollars, and I had to throw it out."

I'm helping a new guy stretch in Tae Kwon Do class, when he gasps, "Christ, I'm beat!"

"Me too," I say. "I get so tired here, I thought I must have AIDS. My psychiatrist suspected Epstein-Barre, but the tests were negative, so he put me on Elavil. That made me impotent and gave me hemorrhoids, which ruled out anal intercourse, so I stopped the meds, but now I'm suicidal half the time."

"Bastards," the man in line behind me at Circuit City snarls as we watch a newscaster announce, on Big Screen TV, "Congress cuts Welfare again."

"I was on Welfare for years," I say. "It supported my drug habit. When I wasn't too wasted, I fathered kids: nine of the little bastards, so to speak. In my spare time, I robbed liquor stores. Now that Swami's turned my life around, I think all Welfare leeches should be shot, or banished at the very least."

This from me, a lifetime liberal Democrat!

"Fuck the homeless," I say. "Fuck their ratty clothes and long faces and sloppy, misspelled signs. We all paid taxes to educate those bums. They should've learned!"

Am I a silence-phobe? Do I dread more than death the stifled yawn as someone thinks, *Six billion people, and I'm stuck next to him?*

Do I fear that my neighbor feels burdened by the need to speak, and so I lift the conversation off his back? Do I feel so unworthy that only by cracking my bones and offering my juiciest marrow will I be suffered to stay?

Am I so guilt-wracked I'll seize any chance to confess anything? Is this my Jungian shadow, that—as opposed to murder, which hides very well—will out? Is the Imp of the Verbose not a metaphor, but a flesh-and-blood homunculus that controls my jaw, larynx, and tongue? Do we create the world through metaphors, and experience that in which we believe?

My cousin believes her boyfriend will marry her. On the other hand, *he* tells me that she's so neurotic and they fight so much, he has to smoke a bowl of "skunk" just to e-mail her.

She subscribes to *Modern Bride,* is choosing china, and hums Mendelssohn's "Wedding March" all day.

When I see her next, what will I say?

Hot Popsicles

Some days he only has the regular, cold ones. Still, he loves roaring down oak-canopied streets, his truck clanging "Night on Bald Mountain" as he shrieks "Hot popsicles!" and the kids who've boiled out of their houses, waving Mom's limp dollar bills, stampede back inside, wailing.

The days his truck plays "Stars and Stripes Forever," he's a hero, trying to make an All-American buck selling popsicles bought cheap because they melted and re-froze. "Hot popsicles," the trade calls them—texture more granular, shape less perfect than ideal; but what do kids care, if the color's there, the sugar's real?

Not hot as in *stolen*—he wouldn't stoop to that!—hot as in *spicy*: Szechuan popsicles, Mexican cayenne popsicles. Hot as in *exciting, explosive, desirable*—hot car, hot wire, hot date—but also the metaphysical, theoretical popsicle that keeps its sex-toy shape while steaming hot as any toddy, cappuccino, or spiced wine: something to lick on a January night as flames pogo in the fire pit, and snow feathers the house.

Ahhh, for a last hot popsicle before bed—solid and sizzling, substantial as those dreams where the lost love-of-your-life comes topless to your birthday party, and you kiss her breasts in front of everyone. You're all adults; sexual attraction is good.

She tastes like hot cherries, perfect for the popsicles I mean.

Superman, Old

He can still fly, and squeeze coal into diamonds, and see through walls and women's clothes; but sometimes, speeding through clouds, he loses control and tumbles like a spent bullet end over end, or forgets where he's going, and has to take a taxi home.

He lives alone—Clark Kent, retired reporter—but believes spies sneak into his room and steal his shoes.

Old *Daily Planets* heap up in his hall.

The Health Department calls about cockroaches. He shoves the inspector through a wall.

When Jimmy Olsen dies, then Perry White, he wants to die too. But Earth has no kryptonite.

Three knives shatter on his wrists. Eight bullets of ascending caliber ping off his skull.

He jumps in front of a train. It derails, killing fifty; he walks away.

His tantrums topple tall buildings. The SWAT Team sent for him retreats with casualties.

The CIA finds Lois in a nursing home. Kidneys shot and colon gone, she says she'll help.

A helicopter lowers her wheelchair into the rubble where Superman sleeps.

She leans down to stroke his cheek. "Superman? It's me."

He jerks upright, eyes baffled. "Old lady—who are you?"

"I'm your mother, Superman," she lies.

His brow softens. "I missed you, Mom."

"Do you remember Lois Lane?" she asks.

He scrunches up his face—still young and handsome as a boy's. "Kinda," he says. "She was pretty."

"Lex Luthor has her. Up there." Lois points at Cassiopeia, glittering. "Can you see her?"

Superman squints. "I don't know . . ."

She takes his hand, still strong as steel. "Lois needs you, Superman. You've got to save her."

"Lois," he whispers, and stands.

She straightens his cape.

"Who are you?" he asks.

"Your mother, Superman. Save Lois. Please."

"Save Louis," he says. Hands above his head, he bends his knees.

"Fly, Clark," she says, then grips his cape, and lets his leap yank her up out of her wheelchair.

Her heart slows as the air thins. Then it stops, her hands relax, and she falls like the last booster of a rocket that, an instant later, starts tumbling end over end toward its home in the stars.

Making Things Right

He's there when I get home: white beard, Charles Atlas muscles—just like in the Sistine Chapel. I feel like Adam when he offers to shake hands.

"God," I say, "You haven't aged a day . . ."

He wastes no time. "You know that test you bombed in tenth grade? The one that kept you out of Honors Math?"

I nod.

"Misgraded! You deserved an A. Remember not making the track team?"

I nod.

"They meant to cut *Chad* Webb. Damn fool coach mixed up the names."

"What about Yale?" I prompt. "Why didn't I get in?"

"Politics." He spits. "One spot was left. You had it. Then the dean's grandson applied."

I shake my head. "I thought I was an utter bleb."

"That's over now. I'm here to make things right." He smiles and nudges me. "Remember Jo Ann?"

How could I forget? I agonized for weeks before I asked her out. She looked me up and down, and said, "'Fraid not, Zit-Master."

Suddenly she's here.

"I was wild for you," she whispers, wiggling down her slinky dress.

I look around. God has discreetly vanished.

"I was scared of sex," she pants. "You were *so sexy*. All the girls were wild for you."

"Thank God," I wake up sobbing happily. "Thank God."

from *Amplified Dog*   2006

Amplified Dog

"What's that?!" whispers my wife.
Through thick layers of sleep, I hear a voice
outside. Distorted. Blaring.

I shuffle to the window. Full moon gleams
on the blue plastic I spread to funnel off
El Niño rains. The night stays still. My feet

leak heat, so I'm moving back to bed
when the voice starts to sing. In Spanish.
Amplified—by what? A blown-out stereo?

"Should we call the cops?" whispers my wife.
"No. It's nothing," I say. Then the dog
speaks: *Woof!*—distorted as the song.

A scene tunes in: A man is swigging Cuervo Gold.
His wife, Dalila's, gone. His heart hurts,
so he pulls out the sound system he's kept

since he sang in Los Pochos, back when he met her.
Maybe she'll hear him from Ramon's,
four blocks away. Maybe she'll throw on

her clothes while Ramon, belly swaying
in pink boxers, can't hold her back . . .
No. So the man lets Paco in.

Tail-wagging Paco: man's best friend.
"She loved you more than me," he says,
and sets the mike to Paco's height. "Call her, boy."

Paco sniffs the mike, then barks, and hears
his voice—*Woof!*—louder than it's ever been.
How many times has he stood in the yard straining

to warn people how much they're messing up?
Woof! Woof! all day. But they won't hear.
They never learn. Hector, as usual, passes out.

Hector—his friend, who couldn't smell trouble
when Dalila reeked of it. Poor Hector, stupid and sad,
just like a man. So Paco calls his warning

as the moon tunnels through black night to silver sky.
Woof! The world you've made stinks to high heaven.
Woof! You're mean to one another. *Woof!*

You let bad people lead you. *Woof!* You work too much,
and don't enjoy enough. You waste your time
on trivialities. *Woof!* Even sex is work for you.

Paco loves the way his voice rattles the house,
then flies off in all directions
like pigeons when he runs right into them.

Ooh My Soul

Little Richard

By night, ghosts roam Aunt Ermyn's
elm-shrouded, hundred-year-old home.
By day, my cousin Pete, just out of high school,
combs his duck-tail and keeps time

to records with his creaky rocking chair.
I'm in the hall, creating all-star teams
of baseball cards when, blaring
through Pete's open door, I hear . . .

war drums? Or is it a runaway train?
Keepa knockin' but you cain't come in,
some kind of preacher shrieks,
then squeals like tires around a curve.

Those chugging drums, smoking piano,
squawking duck-call saxophones
make me feel like an oil rig ready to blow.
I see wells pumping, teeter-totters bumping,

giant turtle-heads working out and in
as bronco riders wave tall hats in the air.
I see girls twirling, dresses swirling
high over their underwear,

guys doing splits, or inchworming
across the floor. It makes me want
to slam my head back and forth
like a paddleball—to jump, shout, bang

my hands on walls, and flap them
in the air—to fall onto the ground
and writhe, flail, roar like Johnny Cerna
in his famous Kiddieland tantrum.

Keepa knockin' but you cain't come in,
the preacher howls. But I *am* in.
I'm in the living room, *Bandstand* on TV,
Dad ranting, "Goddamn Congo beat!"

I'm in the back seat of his Ford
a decade later, learning what that beat
could be. I'm in my first band, hoarse
from screaming "Long Tall Sally."

I'm in my college dorm, trying to jam
that wild abandon into poems.
I'm in my car, heading for work
when *Good Golly, Miss Molly!*

catapults out of my Blaupunkt stereo.
I'm walking into Pete's bedroom,
where I've never dared to go. Oh,
womp bompalumomp, a lomp bam boom!

I'm not thinking in words, but I know
I've spent my seven years rehearsing
how to feel this way. It's more exciting
than a touchdown any day, or a home run,

a gunfight, hurricane waves at Galveston,
a five-pound bass on a cane pole.
"What is that?" I holler. Pete says,
"Rock and roll."

My Wife Insists That, On Our First Date, I Told Her I Had Seven Kinds of Hair

Straight, frizzy, chest, nose, pubic . . . what was I thinking?
Seven is special, I know. Seven thieves. Seven
wonders, sleepers, worthies, gables, cities, seventh

sons of seventh sons with more mojo than seven men.
We ate at Mogo's, I remember, where we chose
from a dozen kinds of vegetables, as well as chicken,

turkey, pork, and beef. The chef spilled our choices
onto a grill, then moved from pile to sizzling pile,
chopped, smoothed, arranged until, with his skilled

spatula, he heaped hot meals into the begging bowls
we both thrust out. I led us to a dim corner,
well aware that of the three body types, six kinds

of laughs, five kinds of breasts, and eight varieties
of lips, hers held the summit of each heap. Her long,
dark hair and sapphire eyes made my hands shake.

Her shape unhinged my diaphragm. I'll bet I groped
in my suddenly dim brain, and spilled whatever
I found onto our talk, I was so eager to keep it sizzling,

so hungry to seem a man whose invention never failed,
well endowed with all good things, including hair.
"At least one kind," I must have meant, "is right for you."

The New World Book of Webbs

I have exciting news for you and all Webbs.

Letter from Miles S. Webb

The brochure shows a boat passing the Statue of Liberty
while its cargo of immigrants stand gaping,
and one small boy—dressed better than the rest—
watches from a director's chair. He,
obviously, is the Webb. Simple but aristocratic.
Poor, but destined for greatness. Set apart

from the Smiths and Joneses, the Rothblatts
and Steins, the Schmidts and Hampys, the Mancusos
and Malvinos and Mendozas and Tatsuis
and Chus, by "the distinguished Webb name."
Excitement steams from Miles S. Webb's letter to me.
The very type leaps up and down. Just buy

his book, and I will learn (I'm guessing)
about Thomas Webb, famous for his kippered
herring jokes, and Jeb Webb of the talking armpits,
and Genevieve Webb, convinced her left
and right feet were reversed. I'll learn the inside story
of Solomon Webb, Dover's greatest circus geek,

and Lady Messalina Webb, transported to Australia
with her husband, Sir Caleb Webb,
son of the merkin-maker Lemmy Webb of Kent.
Best of all, inside the bonus *Webb International Directory*,
one among 104,352 Webb households in the world,
there I'll be: the very Webb who woke this morning

at 5:53 when his new sprinklers ratcheted on
with the screech of strangled grebes—the Webb
who lolled in bed, loving the artificial rain, then cracked
his drapes and saw fat drops anoint his porch,
and a hummingbird light on a hair-thin twig,
then buzz away when the sprinklers hissed off.

The lawn lay drinking, then—each blade
with its own history, each listed in the Book of Heaven
(Grandma Webb from Yorkshire used to say),
each destined to be cut later this morning by José,
one of 98,998 people to bear (*his* letter states)
the "brave and glory-dripping name Cortez."

Pumpkin Envy

How many hours did I lie in bed, thought stapling
my sixteen-year-old arms to the sheets,
thought's curare, when I finally dialed Tami Jamison,
numbing my lips too much to speak?

How often did I think, "I'm dead," feeling
my strength leak away, phlegm drown my lungs,
sarcomas thrust like red toads up out of my skin
in the three days between the blood-drawing

and the doctor's benediction: "Negative."
Thought is a rope that pulls the kite out of the sky—
a cramp that locks the boxer's chin as fists hiss
toward his head. "What sharks?" my friend demands,

launching the sea kayak that gives him so much fun.
How many odes would Keats have traded for one
night with Fanny Brawne? What did understanding do
for Nietzsche, but make him more insane?

Thought is more deadly than crack or heroin.
Its pipe to my lips, its needle in my vein,
I loll in my dark room, and envy pumpkin vines.
Whatever's in their way, they overrun. Unafraid

of blight, birds, drought, or humans' being,
they stretch out in the heat, let their roots drink deep
and—never giving a thought to anything—
make a million copies of the sun.

Cat Possessed by Poet Keats

Cockney John could have sneaked in while Mr.
Meepers lay unconscious with an abscess
At the vet's. Or did the surgeon-poet
Squeak in later, through the draining tube
Stuck in the poor cat's head? It's certain

That—stretched in my lap, my hands conducting
The concerto of his purr—he said,
No, no, go not to Lethe, neither twist
Wolf's bane, tight-rooted, for its poisonous wine.
Within a week, he'd rattled off "Endymion,"

"The Eve of Saint Agnes," "La Belle
Dame sans Merci," plus all the odes.
He liked to sit with Kate and me, watching
Clouds dirigible across the sky,
The sun's last rays igniting them

As mockingbirds extemporized. Kate recognized
The most melodious pair: Felix and Fanny
Mendelssohn. Toadily, Kate's southwest
Toad, turned out to be Georgia O'Keefe;
Nigel the Hedgehog was Shakespeare;

Tchaikovsky, Yeats, Bach, and Vermeer flocked
To my back yard, chattering. Even
The caravans of ants proved to be artists,
Though minor ones, like me. First
Among us all was Keats, making us laugh

With his "Mra-*raa!*" and "Tee Wang Dillo Dee,"
The "amen to nonsense" which he used
If I got pretentious, fought with Kate
Over trivialities, or didn't pay
Attention as he caught flies, chased pink

Ribbons, wrestled his jingling mouse.
It was Keats, I know, who called the others
To my house, and convinced Kate to marry me—
Kate, whose love offsets my lack of genius,
And makes me capable of anything.

Prayer to Tear the Sperm-Dam Down

Because we need to remember
that memory will end, let the womb remain
untouched.

From "Prayer to Seal up the Wombdoor," by Suzanne Paola

Because we know our lives will end,
Let the vagina host a huge party, and let the penis come.

Let it come nude, without a raincoat.
Let it come rich, and leave with coffers drained.

Throw the prostate's floodgates open.
Let sperm crowd the womb full as a World Cup stadium.

Let them flip and wriggle like a mackerel shoal.
Let babies leap into being like atoms after the Big Bang.

Let's celebrate fullness, roundness, gravidity.
Let's worship generation—this one,

And the next, and next, forever.
Let's adore the progression: protozoan to guppy

To salamander to slow loris to Shakespeare.
Forget Caligula. Forget Hitler. Mistakes

Were made. Let's celebrate our own faces
Grinning back at us across ten thousand years.

Let's get this straight: Earth doesn't care if it's overrun—
if it's green or brown or black, rain forest, desert, or ice pack.

A paper mill is sweet as lavender to Earth,
Which has no sense of smell, and doesn't care

If roads gouge it, or industries fume into its air.
Beetles don't care. Or crows,

Or whales, despite their singing and big brains.
Sure, rabbits feel. Spicebush swallowtails

Feel their proboscides slide into flowers'
Honey-pots, which may feel too,

But lack the brains to care. Even if beagles
Are mournful as they look—

Even if great apes grieve, wage war, catch termites
With twigs, and say in sign language,

"Ca-ca on your head," they still don't care.
Or if they do—well, join the club.

We humans care so much, some of us dub life
A *vale of tears*, and see heaven as oblivion.

Some pray, for Earth's sake, not to be reborn.
Wake up! Earth will be charred by the exploding sun,

Blasted to dust, reduced to quarks, and still not care.
If some people enjoy their lives too much

To share, let them not share. If some despise themselves
Too much to reproduce, let them disappear.

If some perceive themselves as a disease, let them
Take the cure, and go extinct. It's immaterial to Earth.

Let people realize this, or not. Earth doesn't care.
I do, and celebrate my own fecundity.

I celebrate my wife's ovaries, her fallopian tubes
Down which, like monthly paychecks,

Gold eggs roll. I celebrate the body's changing.
(Might as well; it changes anyway.)

I celebrate gestation, water breaking,
The dash to the hospital, the staff descending,

Malpractice policies in hand. I celebrate
Dilation of the cervix, doctors in green scrubs,

And even (since I won't get one) the episiotomy.
I'll celebrate my bloody, dripping son, head deformed

By thrusting against the world's door.
Let it open wide for him. Let others make room for him.

Let his imagination shine like God's.
Let his caring change the face of everything.

The Animals Are Leaving

One by one, like guests at a late party,
They shake our hands and step into the dark:
Arabian ostrich; Long-eared kit fox; Mysterious starling.

One by one, like sheep counted to close our eyes,
They leap the fence and disappear into the woods:
Atlas bear; Passenger pigeon; North Island laughing owl;
Great auk; Dodo; Eastern wapiti; Badlands bighorn sheep.

One by one, like grade school friends,
They move away and fade out of our memories:
Portuguese ibex; Blue buck; Aurochs; Oregon bison;
Spanish imperial eagle; Japanese wolf; Hawksbill
Sea turtle; Cape lion; Heath hen; Raiatea thrush.

One by one, like children at a fire drill, they march outside,
And keep marching, though teachers cry, "Come back!"
Waved albatross; White-bearded spider monkey;
Pygmy chimpanzee; Australian night parrot;
Turquoise parakeet; Indian cheetah; Korean tiger;
Eastern harbor seal; Ceylon elephant; Great Indian rhinoceros.

One by one, like actors after a play that ran for years
And wowed the world, they link their hands and bow
Before the curtain falls.

A Meal Not Eaten

"Somewhere there's an uneaten Chinese dinner with our name on it."

Overheard

The wonton soup drifts in warm fog
just out of reach. Dragons circle
the bowl as if to guard the one
pink shrimp that bobs like a dead
monster-from-the-deep. Steam

wisps off the twice-cooked
pork and chopped *bok choy.*
The Emperor's Chicken is here too:
sliced peppers, red and green;
black mushroom-gongs; white

meat glistening in glaze. We feed
each other between kisses, screened
by our red leather booth, ignoring
vines that loop and dangle
overhead, the waiters gliding

back and forth, so unobtrusive
it's as if platters fly solo through the air.
One floats toward us, bearing
orange-halves offered
in their bowls of pebbled skin.

Fortune cookies' brittle purses enfold
futures that, like this past,
never occurred. I didn't pay
the bill, open her door, or drive her
to my house, where we never

made love in this bed where I lie now,
in which I can almost touch her,
asleep beside me as my wife,
though she is not, and hasn't been
for a long time.

A Grand Opening of Hearts

Kate and I play Mozart for Erik, read him
Mother Goose, show him *Starry Night*,
wheel his stroller through Descanso Gardens,
pointing out ducks, squirrels, koi,

a basking terrapin, as well as trees, roses,
grass, a lily pond, the sky's vast blue mobile
hung with clouds "like your stuffed animals."
He flails his limbs, and squalls.

Baffled by this grub, this homunculus
who caricatures me, I pitch my voice as close
as possible to his (its timbre gouged
into my brain), and voice my frustration: "Aaah!"

He looks surprised, then replies, "Aaah!"
I repeat "Aaah!" He says it back.
His hands punch with excitement.
I assert, "Aaah!" "Aaah!" he agrees.

It's not Plato & Socrates,
but it *is* flight across a sea-sized
chasm of consciousness. It is
a confluence of minds, and a Grand

Opening of hearts. And it gives rise
to another first for him (but not a last
if I have any say in the matter, any "Aaah!"):
an upward curving of his lips

that evokes the same from me,
as when two friends, long separated,
waiting for takeout in a strange city,
happen to look up, and their eyes meet.

The Open-Air Recital Survived a Shaky Start

when, in the first movement of the *Emperor Concerto*,
where Beethoven tries to out-swagger Napoléon,
a woodpecker countered with Bronx cheers.
Next, every sprinkler in the grassy
amphitheater squeaked on, and listeners fled
as if the Little General's cavalry
had thundered, sabers flashing, from the woods.

The "Rondo" took a whupping, too,
when a squirrel in the oak that spread
above the stage, banged acorns off the soloist's head
and his ebony Grand. The setting sun
scorched through dark columns of trees
behind the stage, as the new soloist marched on.
Her blonde hair glowed, angelic as the tones

she drew, just tuning, from her violin.
We strained forward as her hands caressed
the wood. She was deep into
Tchaikovsky's *Canzonetta*, where he mourns
his unconsummated marriage, when a woman's voice
rose from behind the trees: "Oh God,"
it trilled, a clear coloratura. "Oh, oh, oh!"

What could the soloist do but keep playing?
What could the conductor do but wag
his baton? What could the damp audience do
but shush our children, pretending
not to hear the woman's sobbing obbligato
merge into the theme? And when the finale
began, *allegro vivacissimo*, and the soloist

lashed her instrument into a gallop,
it seemed natural that the woman's cries
should intensify, and the soloist draw strength
from her as together they approached
that last exhausting run up the scale of passion
toward the summit from which, gasping
and quivering, they flung themselves.

When, paroxysms done, the conductor
dropped his hands, and the violinist (on whose
slim legs, seen through her violet gown, I could
have played a pretty tune) lowered her bow,
the applause that surged up out of the soaked grass
was for the woman in the woods as much
as for the soloist: head bowed, smiling. Spent.

How to Live

I don't know how to live.

Various poets

Eat lots of steak and salmon and Thai curry and mu shu
pork and fresh green beans and baked potatoes
and fresh strawberries with vanilla ice cream.
Kickbox three days a week. Stay strong and lean.

Go fly-fishing every chance you get, with friends
who'll teach you secrets of the stream. Play guitar
in a rock band. Read Dostoyevsky, Whitman, Kafka,
Shakespeare, Twain. Collect Uncle Scrooge comics.

See Peckinpah's *Straw Dogs,* and anything Monty
Python made. Love freely. Treat ex-partners as kindly
as you can. Wish them as well as you're able.
Snorkel with moray eels and yellow tangs. Watch

spinner dolphins earn their name as your *panga* slam-
bams over glittering seas. Try not to lie; it sours
the soul. But being a patsy sours it too. If you cause
a car wreck, and aren't hurt, but someone is, apologize

silently. Learn from your mistake. Walk gratefully
away. Let your insurance handle it. Never drive drunk.
Don't be a drunk, or any kind of -aholic. It's bad
English, and bad news. Don't berate yourself. If you lose

a game or prize you've earned, remember the winners
history forgets. Remember them if you *do* win. Enjoy
success. Have kids if you want and can afford them,
but don't make them your reason to be. Spare them that

misery. Take them to the beach. Mail order Sea-
Monkeys once in your life. Give someone the full-on
ass-kicking he (or she) has earned. Keep a box turtle
in good health for twenty years. If you get sick, don't thrive

on suffering. There's nothing noble about pain. Die
if you need to, the best way you can. (You define *best*.)
Go to church if it helps you. Grow tomatoes to put *store-
bought* in perspective. Listen to Elvis and Bach. Unless

you're tone deaf, own Perlman's "Meditation from *Thaïs*."
Don't look for hidden meanings in a cardinal's song.
Don't think TV characters talk to you; that's crazy.
Don't be too sane. Work hard. Loaf easily. Have good

friends, and be good to them. Be immoderate
in moderation. Spend little time anesthetized. Dive
the Great Barrier Reef. Don't touch the coral. Watch
for sea snakes. Smile for the camera. Don't say, "Cheese."

New Poems

Shadow Ball

Let's say some black guys in the '30s hustled up a baseball game;
then right away this tree-trunk-armed Josh Gibson type
lambasted their one soggy Spalding-with-its-cover-falling-off
past the sasparillas into Okeefokee Slough. Next play,
the pitcher wound up, and threw a fat nothing. The batter
swung, and smoked a low line drive the shortstop blocked,
then fired to the first baseman, who did a split and scooped
nothing out of the dirt just as the runner banged the bag.
"Out!" roared the umpire, and both benches cleared.

The Pittsburgh Crawfords, Birmingham Black Barons,
New York Black Yankees—even the Indianapolis Clowns
beat the best white teams at real baseball. Still, before a game,
they'd whip around-the-horn that spherical hunk of the void
they knew so well—slamming it deep, chasing it down
so skillfully few whites who saw them guessed the trick.
Black folks were shadows to most white ones anyway,
though we whites pioneered the shadow services
for which government is famed, and the shadow intelligence

that dims high offices across the land, not to mention
shadow marriage, where couples make real mortgage
payments to shadow companies for shadow homes,
have shadow sex, and before they sleep with shadow partners,
say "I love you" without the shadowiest notion
what they mean, which is why their kids prefer the well-
lit screens of movies and the World Wide Web
to baseball, and professional theorists swear there's no *real*
life, *real* excellence, *real* meaning, real *real*, and the most

enlightened answer to "Good night" is, "*Good* is a race-/
class-/gender-determined abstraction. And it's not night.
The sky just looks that way." Yes, it looks darker every day.
Those Negro League all-stars—Oscar Charleston, Willie Wells,
Buck Leonard, Cool Papa Bell—who couldn't stay in white
hotels, eat in white restaurants, or play in the so-called
Major Leagues, but who apparently enjoyed life anyway,
can be forgiven if they laugh in their all-black graveyards
to see shadows reach out black gloves and grab us all.

Comebacks

The Eagles pack houses each time they return—but smaller
houses, the ones who pack them, grayer every year.
Once a month, Zeppelin's Jimmy Page kicks smack,
and picks up a new singer, though none achieves

the stratospheric shrieks of Robert Plant in '69. *His
comebacks scare me: gullied face and raven *grak* . . .
Roy Orbison's voice was sweeter, his throat more relaxed
than in his prime, the day a heart attack yanked him off

the comeback trail for good. The Rolling Stones refuse
to roll away. But like drunks in bars who won't stop
yakking—like exes who must be dragged, weeping
and thrashing, off love's stage—the saddest comebacks

end with no place left to go. The boozy guitar man
slumped next to me in Denny's can't believe he's laid down
his last Number One, dumped by a boy who runs his record
company the way he totaled Daddy's Testarossa. Oh,

it's easy to sneer, "Why can't the whiner just stride proudly
into that dark night?" Easy to hoot, when no crowds howled
"Encore!" for you. Easy to love the nosedives of the great,
driven lower by their heights than we who fight to keep alive

the joys of Maui in '95, the thrill of Joan in '59, that song
with Frank—"Minnie the Moocher"—mired in Germany, 1944.
But don't all of our bands break up, our shows shut down,
agents stop returning our calls? Isn't every song, poem,

novel, painting, snapshot of a friend, a plea? Johnny,
come back. Come back, cherry-red Datsun with candy-
striped canopy. Thirty-inch waist, come back. Bring more
of your Hershey kisses, Carla, to Oaks Drive-In,

Horror of Dracula receding as, in the back seat of Dad's
gray Ford, we settled down to feed. Wake me to oatmeal
and toast with cherry jam, my clothes laid out, my Tarzan
lunchbox packed—oh Mommy, Daddy, please. Come back.

Blues

I've slipped out early from the Jersey
summer home where my family's vacationing
with Auntie Liz and Uncle Duke,
whose black Lincoln stinks of cigar,
and who, Dad says, is "rich as Crease-us,"
who Dad says is "rich as Crease-us."

Fog squirms its way inside me as I squinch
across the sand, gripping my four-foot
fishing rod: same height as me.
I'll dig sand fleas, then wind my hook
through their shells stuffed with orange guts—
brittle shells stuffed with orange guts.

But sand flea territory is awash in men
with hip boots, surf-rods tall as trees.
Their casts soar seaward, high and deep
as Mickey's drives to center field.
The air froths with their home-run cries.
The air froths with their home-run cries.

Behind them, on dry sand, long
silver-blue fish thrash away their lives.
Cold seawater gnaws my knees
as I wade to cast my half-ounce sinker
and bare hook—Whirr-PLOP!—
my bare, unbaited hook—Whirr-PLOP!—

into the dirty chop ten feet from me.
Men tromping back and forth ignore

this boy who picks at his backlash,
blubbers, and prays, *Please
Mister Bluefish, bite my hook. Please
Mister Bluefish, bite my hook. Please*

*God—I'll mind Mom, and give Junie
half my trucks. Dear Devil, please,
I'll cuss, and copy Reed White's tests,
and steal from the collection plate
on Sundays if you let me catch just one.
Please let me catch just one.*

Sometimes I dream a big blue tows me
out to sea. I wish I hadn't wished
so hard, when breakers high as Everest
swamp me just before I wake in bed.
On that day, though, I stood for hours,
chewed by surf. I stood for hours

chewed by surf while giant bluefish
boiled around me as I cast and cried,
reeling in *Too small, too weak,*
and *No mercy from big men—*
reeling in *Can't catch a break,*
reeling in *Can't catch a break,*

and *Luck passes me by*: things Dad said,
holding up his life to Uncle Duke's—
things that were true, and always would be,
any fool could see, that day.
True, I knew—and always would be—
as Dad dragged us home that day.

Sneaker Males

Big Bo the Beetle digs a burrow under a prime heap
of howler monkey dung, fills it with females, then guards
the threshold, brandishing a horn as big as he is;
yet nub-nosed Sylvester tunnels into Bo's estate
and mounts Bo's females as His Enormosity does

the oblivious dance called *I'm the One.* So genes
of sneaker males survive. Tone-deaf canaries.
Deer with pygmy racks. Cuttlefish so low on male
mystique they wear drab, female hues, mix with the Big
Gun's girls, then, when His Studliness turns

his rainbow-pulsing back, dart in to sneak some female
a packet of sperm. So every man is not six-nine
with a brick chin. My three-six son, watching *Smackdown*
on TV, flexes and struts, then body-slams the teddy-
bear Grandma sent for cuddling. "You want

a piece of me?" he shrills, and leaps on Kid Bear
while I cringe. How long until Kid Bear is me?
If only God had made me Heavyweight Champ,
as I used to pray. Still, Tall Mike Ball, who dragged me
through Taft Junior High's halls in my jockstrap,

got shot to death robbing a liquor store. Dallas Brandt,
Waltrip High's All State tailback, sports a frog belly,
and runs a laundromat, while I boast an Alpha job,
A-list wife, and All Star son because, years back,
like Sergeant Wimply of the Yukon, I failed to get my man.

He played guitar, had long blond hair and "connections"
(my girlfriend gushed) "to Aerosmith." "Just a friend,"
she claimed. But when her roommate said, "She's
at the library . . ." then stumbled over "studying," I slipped
my Boy Scout hatchet in my belt, and went hunting.

Back in high school, I'd played astrologist, the better
to trade horoscopes with Cyndy P. while Detective Daddy
grilled me from the den. Helping Marti N. with algebra,
I encouraged her to whine about football heavy
Blake B., and felt her breasts when x would not

be found. That night, though, I prowled the stacks
like Bo, who's heard suspicious scuffling and, horn
buffed and ready, comes. Rage and pain had swollen me
to Alpha size when, sure I saw them, I yanked
my hatchet out. But the couple kissing in the dust

of British lit were startled strangers. Nor did I find
the traitors in the parking lot, though I peered in
every car window before I drove home sobbing,
threw myself in bed, and woke next morning in the small,
familiar body I wear now.

Goddess

Did she fall from the sky, a meteor miraculously spared by Earth's
　　insipid atmosphere?
Did she rise from the sea: coincidence of elements and ancient
　　lightning?

They say film studios attract her. They are, as usual, wrong;
　　studios spring up at her feet.
I met a goddess on an airplane. She was reading *Travel World*,
　　and kept us all from plummeting out of the sky.

A man married a goddess. Each morning he bathed in chalk dust,
　　and could not say why.
A woman lay in wait to kill a goddess; but her .45 shot out a rose-
　　and-hyacinth bouquet.

In Beverly Hills, CA, the average person spots a goddess once
　　a week.
In Humptulips, Washington, it happens once a lifetime, and she's
　　leaving.

Men see a goddess, then go home and beat their wives; women see
　　one, and claw at their own eyes.
A plastic surgeon makes a false goddess. Only her baby isn't
　　fooled.

The getaway car broadsides a minivan. A mother's skull is
　　crushed.
Her children scream as two big cops throw up. No goddess can
　　be found.

Monks in robes the color of dried blood curse the goddess, hurling
      communion wafers soaked in holy water
at "foul sins" they see "swooping like bats around her in the throbbing
      air."

Watching us watch her, our leaders quail. "Back to your TVs,
      your MasterCards
and demolition derbies," they scream as their accomplishments
      shrivel in our stare.

Slice off your knees; the goddess wearies of your homage. Chop
      off your arms;
she tires of your embrace. Pull out your tongue; she sickens from
      your lies.

In case of air raid, the goddess yowls like a siren. In case of fire,
      she clangs like a bell.
In case of earthquake, she stands where everyone can see her
      jiggling.

When a goddess dies, her memory is a sun suspended on a chain
      of gold.
When a goddess runs off with another man, she leaves a black hole
      just the size to swallow you.

Feeders

When he asks why her daughter's crying, Barbara says,
"One of her turtles killed the other ones. Look there!"
Thick gray limbs, spotted pancake shell, plesiosaur neck—
the killer swims back and forth, up and down a murky tank
brightened by layers of pink gravel and black rock.

Barbara's forty-nine, and shows every hour: face lined,
weight settling like cereal in a box. Her daughter, Crystal,
has the looks her mother's lost. Her weeping seeps
underneath her bedroom door, childish and womanly:
shrill cries; husky gasps and moans. His own mom cried

that way the day his football smashed Grandmother's vase—
as if her heart were being torn out through her eyes.
The keening rises. Like a baby's, but with grown-up heat.
As Barbara lists places to eat, he pictures Crystal on a pink bed,
ringed by plush kittens, hearts dappling the sheets.

Such beauty shouldn't suffer, he thinks, knowing beauty
has no privilege with pain. Still, Crystal will find lots of men
to comfort her, while Barbara finds fewer every year.
Isn't that why *he* is here, trying—while he has some good
looks left—to snap up a partner for the long decline?

"She dumps cute little goldfish in the tank," Barbara says,
almost loud enough to drown out Crystal's cries.
"*Feeders*, she calls them. That reptile chases them around,
shoots out its lizard neck, and chomp!—it gulps
them down. That's their life's purpose: feeding him."

Crystal's sobbing shakes his gut the way one chord
strummed in a music store starts every other guitar
rumbling. He's afraid he'll drop down on the threadbare rug,
and howl—howl for his marriage, its last fireball
of hate; howl for his parents' old-age degradation;

howl for his womanless home, the chipping
paint and leaky sink and jammed back door; howl
for the burned in paramedic vans, the *desaparecidos*,
Chinese earthquake victims, children starved in Africa—
all the sob-stories he tries to mock before they suck him in.

"If you need to stay with Crystal . . ." he begins. "No,"
Barbara snaps. "She needs to deal with losing things."
Out on the street, a car blasts gangsta rap. Its drive-by
bass hammers his brain. Sun glints off Barbara's white
stucco house, black burglar bars, thousands of small red

flowers like open mouths or wounds among the green
ice plant that overruns her yard. As Barbara sighs, and turns
to close (too hard) her door, he knows it's his imagination,
but he'd swear the turtle stops scouring its tank for feeders,
smiles at him, and winks one yellow eye.

Big

I know when I buy it that it's big. And when the guy
who wheels it out, not on a dolly, but a flatbed as long
as my truck—when that guy, with his Fu Manchu

and lifter's belt, won't try to lift it, even with my help,
I know it's *really* big. And when the guy *he* calls
clumps up, and as he cinches on *his* belt, I shove,

and the thing won't budge, I know it's *too* big. Not
until, though, we hoist one edge onto my tailgate,
and for an instant, half its weight presses my knee

so hard I feel a bruise rising, straight-edged as the box—
not until then do I grasp half how big it is.
My fantasy—family and friends watching theater-style

movies in my den, popcorn and cappuccino courtesy
of me—collapses like my dream of surfing Malibu.
Somehow I thrashed to where the surfers bobbed,

relaxed as gulls on the broad-shouldered swells.
But my wave didn't break into a two-foot roil of chop
the way Galveston waves do, as if the sea has unrolled

a frothy white rug. It kept rising—a titanic
shoulder shrug—and I knew it was too much wave:
too much mass, too much speed, too much water.

It was too much wrestler for me, too much marlin,
too large an army with too many missiles raining down.
It was too much fastball, too much free fall,

too many tacklers, too few blockers, too many rules
of etiquette, far too many lawyers slithering into town.
It was too much thermodynamics and windchill,

too much calculus, too much interest on a mega-jumbo loan.
It was despair, genital shrinkage, intestinal outrush,
earthquake on top of earthquake grinding me. Oh,

it was fear, fear, fear. I know, as that big TV crushes down,
I'll never make it do my bidding, or give me back
what used to be my home.

Kidnapper-Couple Who Forgot to Leave a Ransom Note Sentenced to 14 Years

Forget the terror of the four-year-old, abducted
by a man who spelled money *mune* in the note he left
in his pocket, scratched in blood because he sharpened
not his pencil, but his thumb. Forget his dunderheaded wife,
who tossed the toast because she'd buttered it on the wrong
side. Ignore the fact that fourteen years is barely time
for them to start exploring, with their pen-light minds,
the Carlsbad Caverns of their own ineptitude. Disregard

the anguish of the mom, who never married her child's
father, or memorized his name, and thought her hooker
friends sat babies too. Throw them all into the joint
with the bank robber who wrote a holdup note on his own
deposit slip, and the john who flagged the cops after some
tranny stole his stash. Don't get your undies in a bunch
about the sub that did an "emergency blow" to impress civilian
guests, and bisected a ship full of students, drowning nine.

Drop that debacle in the same dustbin with power
"deregulation," airline (in)security, aerosol cans,
infernal combustion engines, and the atmospheric-nitrogen-
to-fertilizer process that has let Earth's population
skyrocket, and will bring it crashing down. Bungling
makes the world go round. The stolen missile
is cancelled by bad aim. The rising of the sea from global
warming is countered by ten million basements flooded

by men trying to fix their sinks. Even if Ebola rides
out of the Congo on some epidemiologist's shoe, so many
people have screwy DNA—so many cells can't get
the genetic code quite right—*Homo sapiens* will survive.

My new house "must have been wired by an arsonist,"
the electrician says. All my *Hot* and *Cold* knobs
are reversed, but at least no rain, snow, or carcinogenic
sun can get to me. Ma Bell may bill me thousands

for a local call routed through Fiji. Doctors may
amputate my leg when I walk in for an appendectomy.
The car-alarm installer may nick my brake line, causing
my safety-first Volvo to dive off a bridge, killing
my family. Still, some mortician will gain three burials.
An antidepressant maker and a crutch company
will add a customer-for-life. The human race will stumble
on.

Teachers' Names

For what more-than-mortal sin is the soul squeezed
into the body of a grub, then forced to enter
a room boiling with teens, and say, "Good
morning, class, I'm Mrs. Butt"? What Malevolence
found the one school in Texas where a penis was a *doan,*
then dumped Mr. Smalldoan in its dusty halls?

My friends and I learned self-control, intoning,
"May I have a hall pass, Mrs. Titsworth, please?"
We learned creativity, finding fresh ways
to pronounce Ms. Birchett and Mr. Fuchs.
Dr. Harold (Harry) Beaver just made matters worse
by brandishing his pointer like a swagger stick.

Drafted from Home Ec. to teach Science, Mrs. Daft
wore mismatched socks, and declared with papal
certainty, "Saturn's bigger'n any stupid star."
What we lost in knowledge, we made up
in hilarity—we with our zits, loving cup ears,
and one-leg-shorter-than-the-other, our dyslexia

before it had a name, our inability to catch
a football or to solve for *x,* our scoliosis and bad
breath, birthmarks, cleft palates, star-crossed eyes.
"Fats," "Retard," "Midget," "Braces"—all of us
could lord it, watching Mr. Cripp clatter to class
with padded crutch handles in red lobster hands.

Scars plastered with Clearasil, we felt our weak
hearts shake our sunken chests with—wasn't it

laughter?—at the substitute's quivery ham-
hock legs and rat's-nest hair. No man would ever
squeeze a ring onto her liver-spotted hand.
She'd be Miss Woodcock till she died.

I Have Much Better Poems than This

They start off better: understated, but attention-grabbing as a headline
    in *Hollywood Star*.
Poignant as cancer-kids, they're sensitive, mature, compassionate,
    and ethical,
Whereas this poem is self-involved as a clap-stricken serial killer being
    fitted with a catheter.

My better poems scorn all comparisons that might induce cheap
    smirks.
They're chiseled words: perfect thought sculptures,
While this poem is—let's be frank—a literary whoopie cushion, or at
    best, a Big Mac with small Coke and fries.

If we must compare my better poems to food, they are meals worthy
    of Escoffier.
They don't hyperextend their elbows and throw out their backs straining
    for fresh imagery.
Details leap from them—sensual, specific—like sardines chased by
    yellowtail through turquoise seas.

This poem may do for an interlude of slit-skirt, push-up-bra, *unh-unh-*
    unh activity; but its edible panties make you wince. No way you
    want to wake with *it*.
Each line surprises in my better poems—surprises, yet seems inevitable.
In *this* poem, I flung in anything that crawled across my brain. A desert
    tortoise crunching arugula, a bougainvillea (San Diego red) wilting in
    heat, an ant bite on my navel . . . even gas pains don't go unexpressed.

I'm saving my better poems for (why mince words?) a better place.
Their endings leave readers both shaken, and stirred to give all their
    possessions to the poor—

To make millions, then found libraries and universities—or quit their jobs
　　　　and be Alaskan fishing guides—or rush into the kitchen and create
　　　　hundred-layer cakes of alternating chocolate, plum preserves, and
　　　　mackerel paste.

This poem barely dares to suggest that reading it is worth missing three
　　　　minutes of the *Nightly Catastrophic News and Group-Weep*—
That it's better than hearing "Born to Be Wild" on the oldies station
　　　　for the millionth time, while you thrash in a cold bed, trying to get
　　　　comfortable.
You should be warm now. Close your eyes. Rest, if you can't sleep.

He Won't Go to Sleep Without Me,

I like to say. I must like to; I say it all the time, leaving
parties early, acting put-upon. My boy sucks the blood
out of my social life, friendships draining like my hopes
to pitch for the Braves, or find important fossils in my yard.

Still, I love knowing my son won't let sleep's towel
cover his head until he hears my tiptoed footsteps,
throws open his door, and squawks, "Daddy! Hug!"
Non-parents may think he's a Mars-sized ball-&-chain—

a tackler like Mean Joe Green rattling my brains each time
I try to throw a pass—a Bungee that, just as I'm set
to plunge into some cool pool of adult delight, yanks me
back to the *Teletubby* night. Jim Sweet described kids just

that way as we fished, up to our onions in trout stream.
His girlfriend, Jan, laughed—high and clear as a coloratura,
frank as two dogs in the street. On their first date,
when a broken high heel dumped her on the floor,

she laughed so hard she peed, then couldn't stand,
since her dress hid the evidence, which made her laugh
and pee some more. She must have loved that story;
she told it all the time, laughing as Jim steamed. Her bathroom

humor no more fit Jim's image of *wife* than his image
of *life* held trusted friends. He'd get suspicious of me,
stay away for weeks, then show up with a book
on brook trout that I had to see. "I've never trusted anyone

as much as you," he said so often, he must have liked to say it.
Wading the Skagit one day, I slipped and current
caught me. Two guys had drowned in the same place,
the same way: their waders filled and dragged them down.

But Jim shoved his new rod at me. "Grab on!"
he yelled. I cracked the rod, but it deflected me enough
to let Jim drag me, half-frozen, to shore.
Another time, at Lenice Lake, a rattler slid across our path.

"Let's go," I said when only slither-marks remained.
Out bulled the secret Jim had kept penned up for years:
"I'm scared of snakes." Big Jim, who'd flown army
choppers, couldn't step where the rattler had been.

So, piggyback, the way Dad used to carry me,
I carried him. Afraid-of-nothing Jim. Never-trust-
anybody Jim Sweet (not his real name) trusted me—
then, afterwards, was certain I'd tell everyone.

After he married Jan and had a little girl, he moved
away, wrote once, then stopped. I think of him
when I piggyback my son to bed: all that hope and trust
and life riding on me.

Flashlight

Point, push the switch, and a circle of light leaps
onto the wall. My little boy leaps at the sight,
hands stretched skyward, shrilling, "Yight!"

"Imagine you're riding a beam of it," I say.
"You go so fast time stops, and your body *turns*
into light." "Yight! Yight!" he screams, and springs

for mine. "Yes, light," I say. "Can you believe
it goes 186,000 miles per second? That's in a vacuum.
In more solid mediums, it slows. Not much,

though, unless you're talking Boze-Einstein
condensate. It won't outrun a Moped, then . . ."
Do lights flash on in my boy's head? I've dreamed

of passing Nature's secrets on to him: our own
two-man bucket brigade. I give him,
now, the inside scoop on lasers and photons,

refraction and rainbows. "Light-deprived
people get depressed," I say, and describe light's
wave/particle behavior, and speak the great

incantation, "$E = mc^2$." "Yight! Yight!" he wails,
and starts to cry. I could cry too, thinking
of atom bombs, so I explain how batteries

excite electrons in the bulb's filament to higher
levels from which they fall, releasing bursts
of light. My boy falls to the floor, screaming—

not with delight. He calms when I hand him
the flashlight. "Hope," he quavers, meaning "Help."
I slide the switch. A white hole flames

onto the rug. My boy crows, "Yight!" and sweeps
the hole across the room. "Yight! Yight!"
He grips the bulb, and sees his skin turn red.

(Is that from blood? I've never known).
"Da-Da," he cries, and orbiting the beam
around my head, follows me outside under stars

remote as the chance that he would ever,
from the infinite dark, flame down to me,
carrying such radiance, such yight.

Acknowledgments

Poems from *Reading the Water,* winner of the 1997 Morse Poetry Prize, © 1997 by Charles Harper Webb, are reprinted with thanks to Northeastern University Press, c/o University Press of New England, and with permission of the author. The author is grateful to the following publications for first publishing these poems, sometimes in other versions:

American Poetry Review ("The Mummy Meets Hot-Headed Naked Ice-Borers"); *Antioch Review* ("Invocation to Allen as the Muse Euterpe"); *Florida Review* ("The Death of Santa Claus"); *Harvard Review* ("Umbrellas"); *Michigan Quarterly Review* ("The Shape of History"); *Paris Review* ("In Praise of Pliny"); *Poetry East* ("Spiders"); *Quarterly West* ("The Crane Boy"); *Southern Poetry Review* ("Peaches"); *Gettysburg Review* ("Broken Toe"); *Virginia Quarterly Review* ("One Story"); *Tsunami* ("Prayer for the Man Who Mugged My Father, 72").

Poems from *Liver,* winner of the 1999 Felix Pollak Prize in Poetry, © 1999 by the Board of Regents of the University of Wisconsin System, are reprinted courtesy of The University of Wisconsin Press. The author is grateful to the following publications for first publishing these poems, sometimes in other versions:

Greensboro Review ("Prozac"); *Harvard Review* ("Someone Else's Good News"); *Nebo* ("Byron, Keats, and Shelley"); *Paris Review* ("Tone of Voice"); *Poetry East* ("Musk Turtle"); *Poetry International* ("Love Poetry"); *Ploughshares* ("Biblical Also-Rans," "Wedding Dress"); *Solo* ("Descent"); *Steam Ticket* ("Losing My Hair"); *Sycamore Review* ("Tenderness in Men"); *Journal* ("Over the Town").

Poems from *Tulip Farms and Leper Colonies,* © 2001 by Charles Harper Webb, are reprinted with thanks to BOA Editions, Ltd., and with permission of the author. The author is grateful to the following publications for first publishing these poems, sometimes in other versions:

Apalachee Quarterly ("Death Comes to the Baby Boom"); *Artful Dodge* ("Socks"); *Barrow Street* ("A Salesman and a Librarian"); *G. W. Review* ("Charles Harper Webb," "Waiting"); *Laurel Review* ("To Make My Countrymen Love Poetry"); *Michigan Quarterly Review* ("To Prove that We Existed Before You Were Born,"); *Pearl* ("Vikings"); *Poetry International* ("Did That Really Happen?"); *Puerto del Sol* ("Waking at 3 A.M.").

Poems from *Hot Popsicles*, © 2005 by the Board of Regents of the University of Wisconsin System, are reprinted courtesy of The University of Wisconsin Press. The author is grateful to the following publications for first publishing these poems, sometimes in other versions:

AKA Magazine ("Judge Frosty Presiding"); *Columbia* ("Rat Defeated in a Landslide"); *Epoch* ("Imp of the Verbose"); *Fiction International* ("Superman, Old"); *Paris Review* ("A Ticklish Situation"); *Pinchpenny* ("To Set Himself Off from the Crowd," "Making Things Right"); *Santa Monica Review* ("Consciousness"); *Sentence* ("Hot Popsicles"); *Wormwood Review* ("Conan the Barbarian").

Poems from *Amplified Dog*, © 2006 by Charles Harper Webb, published by Red Hen Press, are reprinted with thanks to Red Hen Press. The author is grateful to the following publications for first publishing these poems, sometimes in other versions:

Atlanta Review ("Prayer to Tear the Sperm-Dam Down"); *Descant* ("Cat Possessed by Poet Keats"); *Georgia Review* ("Ooh My Soul"); *Kansas Quarterly* ("The Animals Are Leaving"); *Michigan Quarterly Review* ("My Wife Insists That, On Our First Date, I Told Her I Had Seven Kinds of Hair," "The New World Book of Webbs"); *Ploughshares* ("Pumpkin Envy"); *Poetry International* ("How to Live"); *Tampa Review* ("A Grand Opening of Hearts"); *Third Coast* ("Amplified Dog"); *Virginia Quarterly Review* ("A Meal Not Eaten," "The Open-Air Recital Survived a Shaky Start").

The author is grateful to the following publications for first publishing these previously uncollected poems, sometimes in other versions:

5 AM ("I Have Much Better Poems than This," "Kidnapper-Couple Who Forgot to Leave a Ransom Note Sentenced to 14 Years"); *Bryant Literary Review* ("Teachers' Names"); *Georgia Review* ("Flashlight"); *Kenyon Review* ("Sneaker Males"); *Michigan Quarterly Review* ("Big," "'Ghost of a Chance,'" "Shadow Ball"); *Pearl* ("Goddess"); *Ploughshares* ("Blues," "He Won't Go to Sleep Without Me,"); *Poetry International* ("We've Got Rhythm"); *Southern Review* ("Feeders"); *Third Rail* (MTV Books) ("Comebacks").

"The Shape of History" appeared in *Best American Poetry, 1995.*
"Prayer to Tear the Sperm-Dam Down" appeared in *Best American Poetry, 2006.*
"Big" appeared in *Best American Poetry, 2007.*

"Cat Possessed by Poet Keats" won the Betsy Colquitt Poetry Award for the best poem; published in 2002 by *Descant* magazine.

"The Open-Air Recital Survived a Shaky Start" and "A Meal Not Eaten" won the Emily Clark Balch Prize for the best poems published in 2003 by *Virginia Quarterly Review*.

"Cocksucker" was first printed, and "Vikings" and "Love Poetry" were first collected, in the chapbook *Dr. Invisible and Mr. Hide*, published by Pearl Editions, 1998.

Several of the prose poems in this book were collected in *Worm*, a chapbook from GreenTower Press, published in 2003.

The writing of this book was partially funded by California State University, Long Beach Scholarly and Creative Activities Awards.

I am grateful to the Mrs. Giles Whiting Foundation and the John Simon Guggenheim Foundation for fellowships that supported the writing of many of these poems.

Special thanks to Aliki Barnstone, Dinah Berland, Richard Garcia, Ron Koertge, Walter Pavlich, Karen Schneider-Webb, Judith Taylor, and William Trowbridge for invaluable editorial assistance, to Phil Levine for giving me a boost when I needed it most, to Larry Goldstein and *Michigan Quarterly Review* for championing my work early and consistently, to Ed Ochester, for incisive editing and the idea for this book, and to Edward Hirsch, poet and teacher extraordinaire, who got the train on track.